HORSE
WISE
G U I D E S

Taking Up
Riding as an Adult

Diana Delmar

STOREY
BOOKS

The mission of Storey Communications is to serve our customers
by publishing practical information that encourages personal
independence in harmony with the environment.

Edited by Elizabeth McHale and Marie Salter
Cover design by Rob Johnson / Johnson Design
Cover photographs © Lisa Helfert
Text design by Faith Hague and Susan Bernier
Text production by Erin Lincourt
Photographs by Lisa Helfert, except where noted otherwise
Line drawings by James E. Dyekman
Indexed by Susan Olason/Indexes & Knowledge Maps

Printed in Canada by Transcontinental Printing
10 9 8 7 6 5 4 3 2

Library of Congress Cataloging-in-Publication Data

Delmar, Diana, 1951–
    Taking up riding as an adult / Diana Delmar.
            p.   cm. — (Horse-wise guides series)
        ISBN 1-58017-081-1
            1. Horsemanship. I. Title. II. Series: Horse-wise guides.
    SF309.D424   1998
    798.2—dc21
                                                    98-25940
                                                        CIP
                                                        r98

Contents

DEDICATION

To Guinness

ACKNOWLEDGMENTS

Many people were helpful in preparing this book, especially the boarders, students, and staff at Woodland Horse Center (Silver Spring, MD), as well as the experts quoted throughout the book who generously gave their time for interviews. Thanks to you all. I am especially grateful to Maggie and Al Brodnick, Tammy Gildea, Paula Moats, Tom Parris, CJF, and Mike Smith, for sharing their knowledge, for patiently answering questions, and for their help in obtaining photographs for the book. Thanks also to my dear friends and riding buddies, Nancy Kassner, Therese Sullivan, and Anne Warner, for their enthusiasm and support.

Riding for Fun and Exercise

A full-time school administrator, wife, and mother of two grown children, Spring Swinehart rode as a child, then took up riding again at age 42. She signed up for once-a-week lessons but so enjoyed the experience that she stepped up the pace and now owns a horse, rides six days a week, and shows.

"Riding gives me tremendous pleasure. It's both a physical and mental challenge. I ride primarily dressage now, and I'm fascinated by the intricacies of movement by the horse, the rider, and their interplay.

I also love caring for my horse. I love his sweet personality, his smell, his feel. It gives me a mental/spiritual lift that affects my entire physical and mental being. Being with my horse gives me a sense of inner calm and satisfaction that I can carry with me. It improves my ability to handle the stresses of my job and gives me a wonderful perspective on life."

▲
Spring and her horse, Nick

L‌ET'S MAKE A WAGER, because I know I can't lose. If you love horses, you want to ride, and if you wisely select a lesson barn, I'll bet you that horseback riding proves to be an immensely gratifying experience that enriches your life in ways you never thought possible.

For many, it's a personal challenge. It requires skill to master control of such a large and glorious creature as a horse, and progress in riding brings a terrific sense of accomplishment.

Riding provides a respite from the hassles of daily life. If you've had a bad day at the office or you've got a case of the blues, go ride a horse and see if it doesn't soothe your nerves, take your mind off your troubles, and raise your spirits.

Interaction with animals is increasingly being recognized as good for our well-being. Horseback riding can help build confidence and self-esteem and improve concentration. It has physical benefits, too, such as improving muscle tone and strength.

Perhaps more than anything else, though, riding is just plain fun. It gives us an opportunity to be outdoors and closer to nature. For many adults, it's a terrific social resource that brings together people of diverse backgrounds who share a common interest. New friends are found not just in people but also in the horses themselves.

Horse Trends

There are currently about 6.9 million horses in the United States, compared with 5.2 million in 1986. Almost 3 million people use horses recreationally, according to the American Horse Council.

How Fit Do You Have to Be?

For an adult looking to take up an exciting, fun activity, riding has a major advantage. You don't have to be an athlete or even have a high level of fitness in order to learn. You might not be able to play a vigorous game of tennis, run in a marathon, or swim ten laps, but if you're in average shape, you can start learning to ride. New adult riders come in all sizes, shapes, and states of conditioning.

Riding might be a bit more physically challenging for some adults than it is for children, but any age-related disadvantages we have usually needn't hinder our riding.

Al Brodnick, an orthopedic and sports physical therapist, explains that with age we lose flexibility, especially around the hips and back. "If you don't have good flexibility in your pelvis and lower extremities," he says, "your seat in the saddle may not be the best. You need to be very centered in the saddle to control everything else." In fact, it may not be the aging process that lessens flexibility so much as it is our lifestyle. For example, many of us have occupations that require sitting at a desk for long periods. Medical conditions such as arthritis also contribute to a decrease in flexibility.

Despite all this, adult riders do have several advantages over children. "Adults' legs are longer, they weigh a bit more, and they process information faster," says Brodnick. If a lack of flexibility puts a damper on your riding, increase flexibility by doing stretching exercises outside of class and before and after each ride.

David Butts, of Windy Willows Farm in Libertytown, Maryland, operated one of the largest stables on the East Coast for about 20 years and was responsible for instructing as many as two hundred adults weekly. He agrees that "adults don't have to be that fit to ride." He does caution that new adult riders should be able to get up on the horse unaided, though he concedes that anyone who wants to ride badly enough eventually figures out how.

Paul Novograd owns three stables in three states, including Claremont Riding Academy in New York, a business that's been in his family for more than 60 years. Like Butts, he has seen a lot of new adult riders come through. He agrees that only a minimal level of fitness is required. For all of us who get glassy-eyed when we think of back-country riding, Novograd says, "Just don't sign up for a weeklong cross-country ride. Start modestly."

If you're a fit person, you're already one step ahead. Chances are you'll find riding easier to learn and you'll progress even faster.

◀
Group lessons give you a chance to meet other people and have fun.

Riding for Exercise

David McLain, a rheumatologist and horseback rider who is active with the American Medical Equestrian Association, an organization dedicated to promoting safe horseback riding, says that when people think of riding, they might assume that "only the horse is exercising, and that's not the case. There are two of you out there working." He says that a study of professional athletes demonstrated that jockeys are the most fit — more so than football, basketball, hockey, baseball, golf, and tennis players. "Of course," McLain says, "racing horses is more physically taxing than trail riding. But riding is good for many muscle groups — the leg muscles, stomach muscles, back muscles, and arm muscles."

Physical therapist Al Brodnick notes that, through therapeutic riding programs, we know riding can help restore the basic elements of posture, balance, and central stability. Certainly, such benefits are good for people of all ages. (See Therapeutic Riding Centers on page 7.)

Horseback riding might even be considered a form of weight-bearing exercise, and studies have shown that weight-bearing exercise can help prevent or minimize the risk for osteoporosis. "If your feet are in the stirrups and you're posting," says Brodnick, "that increases weight bearing throughout the lower extremities and pelvis. Posting also requires motion that strengthens the legs." According to Brodnick, if you trot and canter vigorously and get your heart rate up, riding will even provide some aerobic exercise.

Energy Expenditure

Just how much exercise you get from riding depends on how you ride and how involved you become in horse care. Johanna L. Harris, editor and publisher of *The Equestrian Athlete* (see the resource section), points out that determining the energy expenditure of any athlete is difficult. The energy demands for a sport change with the effort put in by the athlete at a given time, the conditions, and the characteristics of the equipment — in this context, the horse — being used.

Examining how much oxygen is used, however, gives a fairly clear idea of how much energy we use for a given activity. (The body uses oxygen at a somewhat constant rate to convert food into usable energy.) Harris explains: "We know there's a relationship between oxygen used and calories burned, so we can look at the calories an athlete burns during an activity to estimate its energy demands."

These demands are classified by the number of metabolic equivalents (METs) required. For example, says Harris, an activity that requires 6 METs demands that you use six times the amount of oxygen you would use resting quietly. The following chart will give you a better idea of METs and their relationship to physical exertion:

LEVEL OF PHYSICAL EXERTION	METABOLIC EQUIVALENTS REQUIRED
Mild	<3
Moderate	<6
Optimal	<8
Strenuous	<10
Maximal	<12
Exhausting	>12

Walking on asphalt at an average pace requires 4.5 METs and is considered moderate physical exertion; jogging at a 12-minute-mile pace requires 7.7 METs and is considered optimal exertion; and splitting wood quickly with an ax requires 16.9 METs. "That's definitely exhausting," says Harris.

Using caloric expenditure data and the results of a European study of elite and advanced horseback riders, Harris has devised a chart showing that horseback riders can approach optimal physical exertion but seldom more.

CALORIC EXPENDITURE*

ACTIVITY	CALORIES EXPENDED	METs REQUIRED
Grooming	525	7.3
At the halt	78	1:0
Walking	168	2.3
Posting trot	420	5.9
Sitting trot	450	6.3
Cantering	514	7.2
Galloping	558	7.8

Data based on a person weighing 150 pounds.

From the chart and what we already know about METs, it's obvious that horseback riding typically provides moderate to optimal physical exertion if you ride at any gait other than the walk. To influence the level of exertion, Harris notes, "there has to be some sort of effort on the rider's part to control body position and the horse's way of going."

So can riding provide all the exercise you need? According to Harris, "To exercise for health and fitness purposes, people should perform an exercise that burns at least 300 calories an hour, every day." (This is in keeping with the 1996 Surgeon General's report on physical activity and health, which recommends at least 30 minutes of moderate physical activity daily, 7 days a week.) "For most riders, this could include grooming, and riding at a pace faster than a walk," Harris says.

However, Harris says most riders don't ride hard enough to keep their heart rate elevated for the amount of time needed to see a true effect on cardiovascular fitness — 20 to 60 minutes, 3 to 5 days a week. On the other hand, she says, "inactivity and sedentary lifestyles are rampant. Some movement is better than no movement. If people are willing to ride but not run, that's all right. They'll still be stronger and more fit cardiovascularly than someone who is sedentary."

Considering all this, most beginning adult riders, even those riding several times a week, probably shouldn't count on riding as a means to lose weight or improve general fitness. But riding *will* provide some exercise. At the very least, it will help keep you active, and that's healthy!

Time Investment

Riding certainly doesn't take as long as playing eighteen holes of golf, but it can be a moderately time-consuming sport. For example, say you'll be grooming your school horse, tacking him up, riding in a lesson, then cooling down the horse and doing a bit more grooming before putting him into his stall. Count on 30 minutes for grooming and tacking, at least 30 minutes for a private lesson (1 hour for a group lesson), and another

30 minutes to cool down the horse and do some post-ride grooming before putting him away. And don't forget to include your driving time to and from the barn. Altogether, you will have spent 1½ to 2 hours (possibly more, depending on how far you need to drive). That's not much more time than many people spend going to their local health club; and in my book, riding horses is a lot more fun.

Many lesson barns have the horses groomed, tacked up, and ready for students; some saddle up the horses but ask students to bridle. If this is the case where you take lessons, each ride may require less time.

But can you make progress by riding once a week? According to Butts, you can improve by riding just once a week — and you're sure to have a good time — but twice a week is preferable. That might be one lesson and 1 hour of practice time. "It's like learning to play the piano," he says. "To learn to play, you need to practice; with riding, you need hours in the saddle."

Physical Limitations

Most of us well into our 30s, 40s, and beyond have minor aches and pains, ranging from an occasionally sore back to a creaky knee. Learning to ride correctly can make you feel better by strengthening your muscles and helping you stay active.

One condition that can be particularly limiting is osteoporosis. In someone with osteoporosis, bouncing around in the saddle increases the risk of compression fractures. Fractures associated with falls are also more likely in someone with osteoporosis, note rheumatologist McLain and physical therapist Brodnick.

As with any exercise program, an adult who has a medical problem and wants to take up riding should obtain permission from a physician. It's also vital that the instructor be fully informed about the condition. If you have any doubts, a physician should be able to help you determine if a regular riding lesson program is appropriate for you.

Therapeutic Riding Centers

Adults with more serious physical limitations or disabilities don't have to forgo riding. Some instructors specialize in teaching adults who have special needs, and therapeutic riding centers that feature *hippotherapy* — the use of horses to treat the disabled — are becoming more common.

The Denver-based North American Riding for the Handicapped Association (NARHA) currently has some 550 member centers nationwide, and the number is increasing as more people recognize the benefits of riding for individuals with disabilities. Most of these centers serve adults and children. According to Bill Scebbi, executive director of NARHA, some are dedicated exclusively to therapeutic riding; others offer both traditional and therapeutic riding programs.

Helen S. Tuel, Ph.D., founding director of the Therapeutic & Recreational Riding Center, Inc. (TRRC) in Glenwood, Maryland, says that people with a wide range of disabilities can participate. These include people with orthopedic conditions such as scoliosis and neurological disorders such as cerebral palsy, as well as those with autism, blindness, epilepsy, and learning disabilities.

Tuel emphasizes that hippotherapy involves more than giving someone a ride on a horse — it's actually a medical modality. TRRC employs physical and occupational therapists and riding instructors to work with the students to ensure that they get the greatest benefit from their riding experience. TRRC is a recognized rehabilitation facility and, as such, many insurance companies cover the cost of therapeutic riding lessons there.

According to Tuel, riding helps build confidence and gives people with disabilities a chance to socialize with others who have the same interests. Riding improves balance. It also requires many of the same muscles we use when walking and helps tone and strengthen muscles.

A woman from Philadelphia with a form of muscular dystrophy has experienced the benefits of hippotherapy firsthand. The illness left her muscles weak, but her physicians felt that her condition would not progress if she maintained the strength she had.

"Riding enables me to exercise more easily," she says. If she exercises the usual way (that is, working in a chair), it's painful. "On the horse, it isn't," she says. "The warmth of the animal is important. It warms my muscles. It's great."

According to Scebbi, of NARHA, anecdotal evidence indicates that riding sometimes helps people with traumatic brain injury to regain their balance and coordination more quickly than would traditional therapies.

Riding can also help people with disabilities gain independence and freedom. For people with leg paralysis, Scebbi says, "the horse becomes their legs. They can get out and enjoy nature again." He tells of a woman with multiple sclerosis who used a wheelchair until she took up riding, which she credits with helping her regain her ability to walk.

If you're an adult with a disability who would like to learn more about hippotherapy, find a therapeutic riding center that is a recognized rehabilitation facility in your state, or contact NARHA to locate a member center near you. Members agree to operate under certain standards, and use instructors certified by NARHA to teach therapeutic riding.

Finding a Therapeutic Riding Center

To locate a therapeutic riding center in your area, call or write the North American Riding for the Handicapped Association (NARHA) at 800-369-7433, P.O. Box 33150, Denver, CO 80233. You can also check out NARHA's Web page at www.NARHA.org.

◀

Adults and children with disabilities can enjoy horseback riding and get needed therapy at a therapeutic riding center.

Finding a Lesson Barn and Instructor

2

Harvey Hoechstetter, a financial planner, took up riding at age 42, and now rides three to four times each week. His favorite riding activity is fox hunting.

"Riding brings to my life the joy of interacting with my four-legged equine friends. Riding also forms the basis of my physical fitness routine, the foundation of my social life, and a mental escape from the pressures of the daily grind.

The common interest in horses has provided me many opportunities to share adventures and friendships with many active, outgoing, fun-loving men and women."

Whthe you take up riding, it's extremely important to select a barn that's appropriate and an instructor who's right for you. If you make a good selection, you'll find riding an enjoyable activity and you'll look forward to your lessons. You'll meet people who share your interests. Doors will open to lots of other activities down the road, many of them horse-related — and many not.

If you make a poor choice in a barn and instructor, several things could happen. You might become bored quickly, or frustrated that you aren't learning what you thought you would. You could become fearful if you are given a horse that's inappropriate for a beginner or if you are pushed to learn too much too soon. A bad choice could also lead you to believe that it's riding you don't like, when in fact it might be the barn and the instructor that just aren't a good fit.

Here's an example. In my late 20s, when I decided to take riding lessons, I hastily picked out a stable from the Yellow Pages because it was close to home. I spent weeks sitting on a decrepit horse in a tiny ring while the instructor lectured endlessly. What I most remember is being bored to tears, and I quit.

Several years later I gave lessons another try, and again selected a barn based on its location. This time, I rotated instructors: One was a gloomy young woman who never cracked a smile, the other was an older man who taught like a Marine drill sergeant and yelled "RELAX!! RELAX!!" Needless to say, I couldn't relax and didn't last long there, either.

I finally went about things in a smarter way. I asked a knowledgeable family friend about the barns in the area. She provided a list of stables and comments about each. I visited a few, but most appealing was the one she described as "the friendly barn."

On a sunny Tuesday morning in June, I went to observe a class. The instructor was teaching a group of women in the outdoor ring to take small jumps. She obviously had a well-planned lesson, controlled the class, and was pleasant. What struck me was that the women in the class were learning and having a great time. I signed up for lessons that day. That was more than seven years ago, and I'm still there, riding with the Tuesday-morning class.

What you want in a barn might be entirely different. Some new adult riders prefer a more serious, less social approach to riding. That's what appeals to them. The point is to shop for a barn that suits you, because most of us don't have time or money to waste.

Before you begin your search for a lesson barn and instructor, though, let's consider why we need to take lessons, because you should be convinced of their value.

Why Take Lessons?

A nonrider at a party was teasing a group of riders with the comment, "You've been taking lessons all these years and you still don't know how to ride?"

Most people just don't realize all that's involved in learning to ride. It requires many things, but first and foremost is communicating with a very large animal. As one instructor explains, "Horses operate on a pretty standard set of signals. You have to learn those signals." In other words, you have to learn what signals the horse understands.

Learning to communicate requires that you develop a good basic set of skills; integral to that is a good balanced seat in the saddle. Some people develop that seat easily; more have to work at it. It's not as easy as you might think.

Through riding lessons, you learn about more than walking, trotting, turning, and stopping. You learn how to get your horse to pick up the correct lead so he can maintain his balance when cantering around a corner, how to move him sideways so you don't whack your knee on that tree along the trail, how to work a gate, how to back him up. All of these movements require a set of different skills — or signals.

You also learn how to problem solve. What do you do when you ask your horse to canter and he trots fast instead? What if you ask your horse to walk and he backs up? Would you know whether you gave the correct signals? If your horse unexpectedly jumps a log in the woods, could you stay on?

Keep in mind that each horse is as individual as each rider is. In lessons, you get the chance to ride different horses and learn to handle different horses. How do you tell if a horse has a sensitive mouth, and what do you do about it? How do you get a lazy horse to go?

The Sensible Approach to Riding

Taking lessons is the only sensible, safe way to learn to ride. You'll learn to tell when a horse is upset and when you or the horse is about to do something that could threaten your safety. If you pick a reputable barn, you'll be given a safe horse and you'll be able to focus on learning. You'll likely progress more quickly than you would if you tried to learn on your own or with the help of a friend who is well meaning but an inexperienced teacher.

The primary reason many adult riders take and then continue to take lessons, however, is that we enjoy them tremendously. Going on with lessons helps us maintain our skills, and with horses it seems there's always something new to learn. At the barn where I ride, we frequently ride on our own outside of lessons, too, but we ride more effectively when we are in class with an instructor who puts us through our paces. I get more exercise in a riding class. When left to my own devices, I just don't ride with the same intensity; I need that direction and push an instructor provides.

How long you decide to take lessons, and how far you want to advance your riding skills, is entirely up to you. At the very least, take enough lessons to learn the basics thoroughly so that you'll be able to ride safely.

Riding Styles

Those of you who don't already know what type of riding you'd like to pursue should read through this section. You'll want to sign up for lessons at a barn where the instructors can teach you what you wish to learn.

Western or English?

The two basic riding styles are Western and English. The association of Western riding with riding the range in the Old West appeals to a lot of people. Many nonriders view Western riding as requiring less skill and as being a less formal type of riding than English riding. Don't be fooled. Accomplished Western riders have to learn just as much and work just as hard as good English riders. And English riding is not always as formal as it appears to be.

There are several similarities between the basic balanced English and Western riding seats. The rider's ear, shoulder, hip, and heel should line up, perpendicular to the ground.

Western riding doesn't involve jumping; English riding may involve jumping, but not always. English riders post — that is, they raise out of the seat slightly and move their hips forward and back to the rhythm of the horse. Some Western riders post also, but Western riders more often sit to the trot.

Western riders use the reins differently — the horse is taught to turn in response to the rein applied to the neck — and they ride with looser reins than do English riders; they have little contact with the horse's mouth. English riders don't neck rein; they ride with a tighter rein and more contact with the horse's mouth. ("Contact" is tension applied by the rider to the reins, which are connected to the bit in the horse's mouth.)

▶
Take up the style of riding that most appeals to you. Both English (left) and Western (right) have a lot to offer.

COMPARISON OF RIDING STYLES

FEATURE	WESTERN	ENGLISH
Seat	Balanced	Balanced
Jumping	No	On occasion
Posting	On occasion	Yes
Rein	Horse responds to rein applied to neck; looser reins than English	No neck rein; rein is often tighter than Western; more contact with horse's mouth
Gaits (walk, trot, canter)	Same	Same
Terms	Often call the trot a jog; canter is called lope; jog and lope are slower than English trot and canter	
Saddle	Horn Intricate, hand-tooled designs Deeper seat than English Heavy (up to 40 lbs for leather; under 20 lbs for synthetic)	No horn Plain Lighter (about 20 lbs for leather; under 10 lbs for synthetic)

The basic gaits are the same in English and Western styles; horses walk, trot, and canter. But Western riders may call the trot a *jog*, and the canter is called a *lope*. The Western jog and lope are slower than the English trot and canter.

The equipment is a major difference between English and Western riding. Western saddles, for instance, have a horn on them; English saddles don't. Western saddles can be works of art, with intricate, hand-tooled designs and silver accents. English saddles are generally plainer in appearance, but many riders still find their sleek appearance beautiful.

Some people feel that in a Western saddle, they have a more secure seat because the design of the seat is deeper than that of an English saddle. The horn on a Western saddle is a nice security feature, because you know it's there to grab if need be — although that's not what's it's meant for. The Western saddle was developed for working and the horn was used to hold a rope. When you develop a good seat, you will be just as secure in an English saddle as in a Western saddle, and if you need to grab something, you can grab the horse's mane. Without a good, balanced seat, you can come out of a Western saddle, too.

For adults, and especially small women, the weight of the saddle is an important consideration — particularly if you must tack up the school horse yourself. Leather English saddles are generally smaller and lighter than their Western counterparts, weighing about 20 pounds; some of the synthetic models weigh under 10 pounds. A traditional leather Western saddle can weigh as much as 40 pounds. One of the reasons I favor riding English is that I prefer a leather saddle, and the English leather version is lighter and less awkward to handle than the Western. On the other hand, there are synthetic Western saddles that weigh under 20 pounds.

Riding Activities

There are riding activities to suit just about every adult with an interest in horses. Trail riding is popular among both English and Western riders. You can go at a slow pace or aim for fast-paced rides.

If you think that eventually you might like to show, there are all sorts of competitions for both English and Western riders at all levels. Many English barns have low-key competitions just for students — called schooling shows — where you can try out your new skills without a lot of pressure to win and get comments from the judges to help you improve. The schooling shows are divided into classes. For instance, in the *Pleasure Class*, riders take their horses through the basic gaits, and the performance of the horse should look — as the class name implies — pleasant. Because it does not involve jumping, this type of riding is known as *flat work*.

Another type of class in English schooling shows is the *Command Class*. You have just a few seconds to get your horse to obey the judge's instructions to canter, trot, halt, back up, or change direction; how you ride isn't judged. Riders who can't get their horses to obey within the allotted time for the transition are eliminated, and the last one left is the winner. These classes are great fun.

In an Equitation Class, the rider's form is judged, not the horse's obedience.

Endurance or *distance riding* is enjoyed by both Western and English riders. It requires going long distances — often 50 miles or more — and checking the condition of the horse throughout.

If you think that, ultimately, you'd like to participate in more advanced riding activities, and you want to ride Western, you could aim for cutting, team penning, reining, roping, barrel racing, or pole bending. *Cutting* means separating out a cow from a herd. *Team penning* is a group activity; three riders separate out three steer from a herd and chase them into a pen. *Reining* involves riding fast in a pattern. *Roping* is chasing down a calf or steer and — what else? — roping it. In *barrel racing*, horse and rider ride in a figure-8 pattern and make fast, tight turns around barrels.

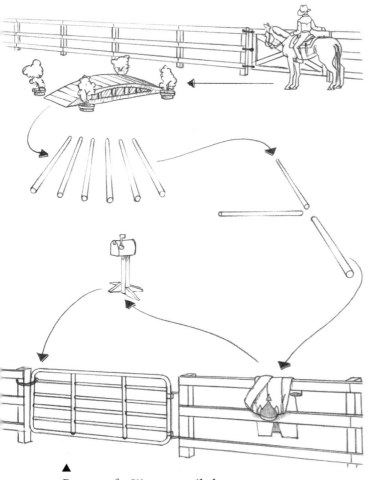

▲
Pattern of a Western trail class

Pole bending is a contest of eleven turns, around a line of six poles that your horse "bends" twice during the run.

Trail classes generally also are a Western activity, although some English schooling shows include them, too. In trail classes, horse and rider negotiate obstacles in a ring. You might open and close a gate while riding your horse, for instance, then walk him across a wooden board, take off a coat and place it on the fence, then back the horse up through poles arranged on the ground in an L formation. Your goal is to show that you can get your horse to obey calmly and navigate over and around objects that might cause other horses to refuse or spook.

Activities considered English riding include cross country, stadium jumping, fox chasing, polo, and dressage. *Cross country* involves taking the horse over obstacles such as logs and ditches in the fields and the woods. *Stadium jumpers* negotiate a series of jumps in a ring. With *fox chasing,* a field or larger group of riders ride hard and fast, making jumps along the way, behind hounds in pursuit of a fox. To play *polo,* riders chase a ball on horseback and try to hit it into the goal with a mallet or polo stick. *Dressage* involves guiding the horse through a series of complex maneuvers with slight movements of the rider's hands, legs, and weight. Watching a dressage horse work is much like watching a ballet.

Some adult riders learn to ride both Western and English. Many ride only one way or the other but learn several activities or sports within that riding style. An English rider, for instance, might learn dressage, stadium jumping, and cross-country jumping; there are competitions, called combined training events, in which the rider can show his or her skills in all three sports. In Western riding events, riders show their skills at pleasure, reining, and trail riding.

▲
A pole-bending horse and rider

◄
Dressage is popular among older riders in part because it doesn't require jumping or high speed, but it still takes a lot of hard work.

▲
A fit adult rider committed to riding in lessons can, with much practice, participate in just about any kind of riding activity he or she wants, including jumping.

Other adults, after learning the basics, choose to perfect their skills in one specific riding activity. Many new adult riders eventually compete; others have no desire to compete but have a great time riding in lessons and with friends. The choices are many; they are up to you.

How Far Can You Go?

Those of us who are average pleasure riders taking one or two classes a week must be realistic about what we can and cannot do. It's unlikely that you'll be a top competitor in stadium jumping or calf-roping, but you can learn to be quite a good rider over time. You can negotiate lower jumps, go on long trail rides, barrel race at lower speeds, and participate in small, less competitive shows.

Among English adult riders, dressage is very popular. It involves hard work and skill but is considered less risky because it doesn't require jumping or high speeds.

The very fit, agile adult rider committed to lessons and practicing several times weekly could, in time, participate in virtually any of the English and Western activities.

Finding a Lesson Barn

Once you know which type of riding interests you, start looking for a lesson barn that teaches that riding style. If you want to ride Western, try to find a stable that teaches Western, and if you know you would like to learn reining, look for a barn that can teach you that, too. If your goal is to learn to ride English and ultimately to learn about dressage, find an English barn that focuses on dressage.

Of course you may not know what you want; then the answer may be an all-purpose barn that offers both English and Western lessons and riding activities. The barn where I have my lessons has mostly English riders, but we have instructors who also teach Western and a few Western riders; the English and Western riders even occasionally take classes together and perform in a team that rides in formation to music. We all enjoy the variety and the opportunity to see how "the other half" rides.

Here's something else to consider as you shop for your first lesson barn: Some instructors recommend that new students initially learn to ride English, no matter what their ultimate goal is.

David Butts, who has taught both Western and English for more than two decades, advises all adults to learn to ride English first. "If they learn first on a Western saddle," he says, "they use it as a crutch — especially the horn — and that's a hard habit to break." Paul Novograd, who owns a number of stables and also has years of experience, believes that it's easier to make the transition from English to Western than the other way around.

Western instructor Diane Schalberg, of Tustin, California, believes everything depends on proper instruction: "If you start riding Western without instruction," she says, "yes, it's easy to plop your butt in the saddle, put your feet up on the dashboard, and go on down the trail paying no attention to balance or feel. If you tried to do that in an English saddle, you'd probably fall off. But with good instruction, I don't think it really matters if you learn English or Western first."

Of course, your decision will have to be guided in large part by what's available in your area. At any reputable lesson barn, you should learn the important riding basics. Just aim for the best match you can between your riding desires and the barns that are available. As Novograd says, "If you really want to ride Western, you probably don't want to be the sole 'dude' at a barn where everyone else is riding off to the hounds."

Talk to Riders

The best way for you to find the right lesson barn is by talking to riders who know the nitty-gritty about the stables in your area. Tell them what kind of riding interests you and explain your goals ("I want to ride Western, learn the basics, and trail ride just for fun," or "I want to pursue dressage and eventually compete"). Then ask which barns they would recommend for adult beginners.

If you don't have friends who ride, speak to people attending horse shows. You're likely to find them a friendly bunch. Speak to the staff at the local tack shops or feed stores. And ask questions!

- Are the instructors good?
- Are the horses safe?
- What's the atmosphere and the attitude toward riding?
- Does it specialize in low-key pleasure riding, or is it a competitive show barn?
- Does the barn have an adult lesson program for beginners? (Some barns primarily teach children and may not have experience teaching adults. And some barns would rather teach more advanced, competitive adult riders than beginning adult pleasure riders.)

Check Out Ads

Another way to start your search for a barn is by glancing at the Yellow Pages or those horse publications you picked up at the tack shop or feed store to get an idea of the stables that are in your area. You can tell a lot from ads. Those barns that welcome new adult riders generally say so. Their ads might say something like, "Classes for adults. Beginners welcome. All you need is a sense of humor." Those that might not be as cordial tend to run ads that don't mention beginners. Instead, they may highlight top-name instructors and awards their riders have won at competitions.

"There is some attitude in the industry," says Paul Novograd. "Some barns tend to be contemptuous of the beginning student. At Claremont Riding Academy, our philosophy is that we love horses and riding and want to share that. It doesn't demean us in any way to teach someone who is new. If we can instill that same enthusiasm in the newcomer, we'll keep them as students. We have the capacity to bring them up to the show ring if that's what they want to do."

Those who plan to ride for pleasure only should seek a barn that's more casual, cautions David Butts, of Windy Willows in Maryland. "If a barn demands you wear expensive boots and britches, it's probably not a casual place. You don't have to spend $200 or $300 to dress yourself for riding. A fun barn will stress a helmet and hard shoes or boots with a heel," he says.

Location

Based on my story about trying to find a lesson stable, you already know that you shouldn't select a barn just because it's the one closest to home. It's worth driving 10 or 15 or maybe even 30 minutes more each way if the barn offers what you want. Don't go to the other extreme, however, and select a stable that is so far away that commuting becomes a hassle. If the stable isn't convenient, you may find it difficult to attend classes regularly.

Size

On your visit, consider the size of the stable. At a larger barn — say with twenty or more school horses and lots of adult riding students — you will be more likely to make new friends. If you are looking forward to taking trail

---

Visiting Barns

Perhaps you're lucky, and you live somewhere where there are two or three barns that sound promising. Call ahead and arrange a time when you can visit. Mention that you'd like to stop by when the person in charge is teaching and available to answer your questions. Also try to visit in the early evening hours or on a Saturday to get a sense of how many people frequent the barn at key riding times, and whether there are other adult riders.

rides with those new friends once you become skilled enough, there's a greater chance that you'll be able to find others to go with when you want to ride. Coordinating schedules among a group of busy adults can be difficult, and it's easier to accomplish when you have more adults to choose from.

A larger barn is also going to have a greater choice of riding times for lessons, and is more likely to have organized activities such as planned trail rides for adult students and shows where students can compete.

There is one disadvantage that comes with riding at some large lesson barns: If you want to get in extra riding time outside of a class, either on school horses or eventually on your own horse, you may have limited access to the rings or arenas, which might be occupied much of the time by formal classes. Be sure to ask whether you will have access to the riding areas at the times you think you would be riding on your own.

Large lesson barns might also have an active children's program, and kids may be running around underfoot. However, a barn that has both an adult and a children's riding program might be a great choice if you are a parent with a child who also wants to learn to ride.

You might prefer a small, low-key barn without a lot of traffic moving through where you can concentrate on your lessons and otherwise find lots of peace and quiet. Only you know what appeals to you — just keep these things in mind as you explore your options.

Facilities

Some of the best lesson barns are not fancy establishments at all, so don't rule out a place just because the buildings need a coat of paint. There are, however, some basic facilities that you'll want to check out. Depending on your riding goals, you'll want to search for a lesson barn that treats its horses and pupils well. And of course, you'll want a barn that has safe facilities.

◄ *A lesson barn with an indoor arena ensures that you'll have a place to ride when the weather is inclement.*

Riding Rings

The barn should have an outdoor ring with soft, even footing, well-maintained fencing, and a gate in good order. This is important to the safety of beginning riders. The outdoor ring also should have lights if you'll be riding after dark. If cross-country riding is your goal, there should be large fields for this purpose.

In a climate where the winter is harsh, you'll especially want a barn that also has a solidly built indoor ring with good footing. Without one, you won't be able to ride at all in the dead of winter when the footing outdoors is so sloppy, wet, or iced over that it's dangerous for both horses and students. In such conditions, barns without an indoor ring will either cancel lessons or provide a "ground lesson," which is more like a classroom lecture. It's good to have some ground lessons, but if that's all you can do for weeks on end, you might become bored.

Trail Access

Do you want to trail ride or take up endurance or distance riding? Ask about access to trails. Good trail access means the barn's property is so vast that it incorporates trails, or that the barn connects directly to dedicated horse trails or bridle paths, and that crossing anything other than a seldom-traveled country road is unnecessary. Dedicated horse trails are just that — they are set aside for riding. This is important for those of you living in fast-growing suburban areas, where development is eating up existing trails, and trail riders are losing the trails they've ridden on for years. Unless the trails are dedicated to horseback riding, or they are on your barn's private property, you could find yourself without a trail to travel. You don't want to have to cross anything other than small, isolated back roads, because crossing larger and well-traveled roads can be dangerous.

To get an idea about the extent of the trails, ask how long it would take to walk and trot all the trails available. If the answer is "about 20 minutes," that means there isn't much trail out there. At some barns, a "trail ride" is considered nothing more than a walk around the property surrounding the barn, and there may not be trails in the woods at all. If you are told it takes "2 hours," or "the entire day" to ride nearby trails, then some nice trail rides are possible.

Ask, too, whether the trails are maintained. A trail that is overgrown with briers and brambles and that has bad footing isn't all that much fun, unless you plan to become a trailblazer.

Are the trails frequented by nonriders such as bicyclists, motorcyclists, and hikers? If they are, you could be in for some hair-raising rides unless the horses are conditioned to accept these encounters.

▲
A well-maintained bridle path is a real pleasure for trail riders.

The Barn

While you're visiting a stable, don't forget to check out the actual barn building. It can give you a good idea about the quality of the facility. The building should be in relatively good order. Stalls should be well bedded with clean material — sawdust, shavings, or straw — and they should not be piled with manure or saturated with urine. (Keep in mind, though, that horses defecate many times daily, so even if a stall was just cleaned, you're very likely to find a pile or two of manure if there's a horse present. A small wet spot among otherwise clean bedding is also to be expected.)

The aisles should be clear of objects other than necessary work items, such as wheelbarrows in use while stalls are cleaned. Each horse should have fresh water.

Ask to get a peek at the tack room. Note whether the bridles and saddles are in good condition. It's unlikely that they'll look new, and they might be dusty because most barns are dusty, but bridles should be free of very worn or weak leather pieces, which could be a safety risk. The saddles should be intact, not falling apart. You want the tack room to be organized, with saddles and bridles hanging in their places.

Horses in pasture should be contained by well-maintained fencing, and they should have water troughs available, unless there is a watering pond or stream in the field.

Horses

Do the majority of horses look well fed and content? They shouldn't be scrawny with their ribs sticking out and the bones in their backs showing. Their coats should look shiny and healthy.

Note I say "the majority of horses," because you shouldn't eliminate a barn because of one or two sorry-looking horses among a bunch of otherwise well-kept animals. A barn can have a very old or ill horse that has trouble maintaining weight or it may have recently taken in a horse that was poorly kept at a previous home.

Checklist for Selecting a Lesson Barn

- ❑ Welcomes adult beginners
- ❑ Offers the type of riding you want to pursue
- ❑ Is located conveniently
- ❑ Has outdoor riding arena
- ❑ Has indoor riding arena
- ❑ Has easy access to trails
- ❑ Has well-kept barn
- ❑ Has well-kept horses

Selecting an Instructor

On your barn visit, ask which instructors teach beginning adult students. Would you have the same instructor most of the time? This is important for continuity. Ask how many years' experience teaching your instructor has, and how long that instructor has been at that barn. You want an instructor available with at least five or six years of experience — usually the more the better — and who has been there for a while, indicating a stable staff.

The person answering the questions is likely to be either the barn owner, the head instructor, or the instructor who would teach you. He or she should be happy to answer your questions. If not, beware! It might signal a less-than-professional attitude about teaching new riders.

Ask, too, what you need to wear. At a good English lesson barn that practices safe riding, one of the first things your instructor will tell you is that you must wear an approved safety helmet and boots with a heel or riding shoes. Traditionally, Western riders don't wear helmets, but in the interest of safety more Western lesson barns are making this a requirement. (See chapter 3, which explains what kind of helmet and footwear you'll need.)

Any well-run barn and good instructor will ask you to sign a liability waiver. Their insurance companies require it.

Instructor Certification: Does It Matter?

There are several organizations (such as the British Horse Society, the American Association for Horsemanship Safety, and the American Riding Instructor Certification program) that certify riding instructors. Some barns have their own instructor-training programs. Generally, a certified instructor will be educated about and have some degree of skill in teaching the fundamentals of riding. These fundamentals meet standards established by the certifying organization. It certainly would be nice to have an instructor who is trained specifically to teach riding.

On the other hand, certification doesn't always guarantee quality. I'm aware of several certified riding instructors who lack practical experience and good communication skills, and therefore aren't effective teachers. I also know several uncertified riding instructors who are fabulous. Before choosing an instructor, try to observe the instructor in a class setting before making your decision.

Instructor Age

At the risk of generalizing, I would highly recommend a middle-aged instructor for middle-aged beginning riders. Not everyone will agree; some lesson barn owners say it depends on the instructor, and of course there are younger instructors who are sensitive to the needs of new adult riders.

However, in my mind, older instructors have several pluses. They probably have had more riding and teaching experience and are more likely to garner our respect. (It's sort of like going to a doctor who is half our age; it's hard to have confidence in her ability if she is young enough to be our daughter.)

I've found that experienced, mature instructors are more sensitive to some of the challenges facing new adult riders: specifically, physical limitations and the fear of injury. For instance, they realize that you might be frightened when learning to canter and won't push you before you are ready and confident.

A mature teacher also realizes that you may not have the stamina that an adolescent rider has, and is more likely to realize when you need a break during a lesson.

Edie Devens, of Trumball Mountain Stables in Shaftsbury, Vermont, a riding instructor and horse trainer with 20 years' experience, readily acknowledges that when she turned 40, her view of what people could do changed. She has become especially conscious of the need to build confidence among new adult riders, which she does by discussing their fears directly and how they can learn to control the horse. She encourages students of all ages to learn and progress, and emphasizes that new adult riders should not be pushed into trying something they aren't ready to learn, either mentally or physically.

So when you're shopping for an instructor, notice whether he or she seems to have some sensitivity to the needs of adults. You might also ask how teachers tailor their instruction to the adult rider.

Observe the Instructor Teaching

Observing a class conducted by your prospective instructor is the single most important thing you should do before committing to lessons. Try to observe a class for beginners.

The first and most significant characteristic you should look for, says David Butts, is whether the instructor is patient and polite to students. You also want an instructor who can maintain discipline within the class.

Good instructors establish control of their class quickly and keep the emphasis on safety. They, and possibly their assistants, will help riders mount. At any good English barn, they will not let anyone on a horse without a proper riding helmet. They will make sure that girths or cinches are tightened, and that horses are safely spaced apart from each other.

Good instructors have their lessons well planned. They will explain what skill they are teaching, they instruct in a pleasant manner, and they are willing and eager to answer any questions that students pose.

They should have a positive, encouraging attitude. They treat students respectfully. They treat the horses respectfully, too, and will never demonstrate any abusive practices, such as yanking on the horse's bit to cause pain, hitting the horse in the face, or kicking the horse.

The most skilled instructors know not to talk too much or too little. They know how much information is appropriate. There's a lot to learn, and if the instructor tries to introduce too much too soon, it can be confusing and frustrating for students.

One of the skills I most appreciate about my instructor Tammy Gildea is her knack for doling out just the right amount of information. She presents us with reasonable challenges in each lesson, accompanied by appropriate instruction. When she pushes, it's within reason. We end lessons on a positive note. We feel we've progressed, but we're also acutely aware of all we still have to learn, so we have a lot to look forward to in future classes. I feel safe in her class, because she knows our fears and limitations. These are all characteristics of a good instructor.

Last but not least, it's nice to have an instructor who is willing to demonstrate. Sometimes, observing your instructor riding is the easiest way to grasp a new skill.

You and Your Instructor

While it's important to like your instructor, don't look for one intending to find a new best friend. It's more important that you respect your instructor. Edie Devens, of Trumball Mountain Stables, explains that to avoid uncomfortable situations and possible favoritism, riding instructors often try to keep their business and personal lives separate. Keep this in mind as you look for an instructor, and try to focus on the person's teaching skills.

School Horse Temperament

While you're observing a class, carefully study the horses participating in the lesson. A good lesson barn will give you the opportunity to learn well, and to do that you need a well-behaved school horse. Although there's always something that will spook just about any horse, good school horses should be what riders call "bomb-proof." They should be the kind of horse that is highly unlikely to rear, buck, bolt, bite, or do anything else that could threaten your safety.

In a class of beginners, the horses should stand quietly when asked to do so. They might shift their weight or swat at flies with their tails, but they should not be dancing around sideways, jumping around raising their front feet off the ground, or sniping at other horses. In general, they shouldn't appear too frisky.

Matching Riding Goals

Before signing up for lessons, discuss your riding goals directly with any prospective instructor. Although a barn may seem to offer what you want, you need to make sure that the instructor will, too. Some instructors don't provide much riding instruction; instead, they are present to enable you to have a supervised, safe ride. Other instructors may want to push you farther than you want to go.

If you're interested in learning to ride so you can meet new people, focus on learning the riding basics and then meander around the trails: Don't sign up for lessons with an instructor who trains riders for competition. You could find yourself in an environment where you don't want to be. By discussing your goals directly with a prospective instructor, you can avoid a bad match and wasted time and money.

Checklist for Selecting an Instructor

Your prospective instructor should:
- ❏ Have at least several years' experience teaching.
- ❏ Conduct well-organized classes.
- ❏ Conduct safe classes.
- ❏ Teach in a pleasant manner.
- ❏ Meet your riding goals.
- ❏ Not talk too much or too little.
- ❏ Welcome questions.
- ❏ Treat students and horses respectfully.
- ❏ Demonstrate when appropriate.
- ❏ Teach in a way that makes you want to join the class.

Lessons: Private or Group?

Whether you should take private or group lessons will depend on the lesson barn and your riding goals, and it's something you should discuss with your prospective instructor.

At the barn where I ride, most adult beginners start in small group lessons with four to six students. Each lesson lasts about 1 hour. You may have to take turns as each student tries out a new skill, such as trotting or cantering, with the instructor observing.

Private lessons often last 30 minutes, although some might be longer. Some barns may even require new students to begin in private lessons.

There are advantages to both types of lessons. In a group lesson, you have the opportunity to make new friends and commiserate about the trials of learning to ride. You can also learn from watching other students.

The major benefit of private lessons is one-on-one instruction. Private lessons may be a must if you need to learn quickly. For example, after the movie *City Slickers* came out, the barn where I ride was inundated with middle-aged men who had signed up to ride in cattle drives out West. Private lessons were their only hope.

Your instructor may advise at least a few private lessons to get you started before you join a group class. Sometimes this is necessary to enable you to catch up with an ongoing class.

Lesson Cost

Group lessons cost less than private or semiprivate instruction. The cost of lessons varies, depending on the region in which you live and the instructor. A 1-hour group lesson generally costs less than a 30-minute private lesson. A 30-minute private lesson with a well-known instructor will cost more. Some riding schools offer somewhat discounted rates if students sign up for several lessons at once.

Lesson Schedules

If you are going to be taking group lessons, find out whether there's more than one adult beginner class available. This is especially important for busy adults whose jobs require frequent travel and who are likely to miss a class here and there. If the only class you can ride in is on a Monday evening, and you have to miss that class one week, you won't be able to ride again until the next week. But if the barn also offers another adult beginner class Wednesday evenings or on Saturday mornings, you can still manage to get in some riding time for the week. Many of you will also find that you'll want to start riding twice weekly or more.

Practice Time

Can you get in riding practice time once you become a student and learn the basics? Some stables allow students to pay or use a makeup lesson to ride a horse outside of a formal lesson (in the ring) to practice what they've learned. In general, this is a good idea once you've had several lessons.

Real-Time Lessons

If you are going to be pressed for time, ask whether the barn will have your horse groomed, saddled, and bridled for your lesson. At a barn that expects students to get the horses ready (after providing training), you'll need to arrive at least 30 to 45 minutes ahead of your lesson. Many barns have the horses groomed and saddled but expect the students to bridle their horses once they've learned how. If getting to class in advance is going to be a problem, consider offering to pay a few extra dollars to have the horse ready for you.

Avoid signing up for lessons at a barn that requires you to get a horse out of the pasture, then groom him and tack him up. This can really be time-consuming. In addition, there are safety practices you need to know before you start taking horses in and out of a field, especially if there are several horses in the pasture. If you have the time and help to do it safely, you may not mind and might even enjoy a walk through the pasture.

In general, however, it's a good idea to learn to groom and tack up a horse for your lessons. Any good rider should know how to do these things, and if you purchase a horse down the road, you'll definitely need to know how. The time spent grooming and tacking up can also be very relaxing, and it helps keep those arms in shape!

Special Clinics

You may want to find out if the lesson barn you are considering offers special riding clinics in addition to regular lessons. These are sessions that bring together students from several classes for extra instruction on a specific skill, such as the sitting trot or the canter. Special nonriding clinics might also be offered on topics such as grooming and understanding horse behavior. In my area, cost for a special clinic is about the same as a group lesson. They're usually lots of fun, so take advantage of these opportunities when you can.

Payment and Makeup Policies

Payment plans are going to vary, but many lesson barns will encourage you to sign up for a series of lessons. They may offer a discount if you pay for lessons a few months in advance, or for quarterly payment. I'd advise paying for 1 month of lessons, if possible, until you are certain you like the instructor and the lesson barn. If you do, then you can pay quarterly to save yourself money. Be sure to ask whether a barn will refund your money in case you must drop out after paying in advance.

If your barn allows you to make up a missed class for no extra charge, that's great, but be aware that some barns require that you use makeups within a certain time period.

Changing Needs

I hope you find a barn that you like, where you can learn much and improve your skills. After taking lessons for a while, though, you may decide that you would prefer another type of riding altogether. Or perhaps the lessons or instructor aren't all that you had hoped. Don't be afraid, then, to make a change or to spread your wings.

---

3 Riding Clothes for Comfort

Nancy Kassner is an archaeologist who resumed riding at the age of 47. She owns a horse and rides four or five times a week.

"As a teenager, I discovered that riding made me forget if I was depressed or upset. As an adult going through a divorce, I realized that riding, more than therapy, would help me through the hard times — and, in the long run, probably would be less costly, too!

Riding provides a perpetual challenge and learning experience. Champ, my horse, brings another dimension to my life, more so than my cats or my dog. There's the challenge of learning how to ride, and of having the horse respond to me. I must be thinking constantly to apply all the tools I've been taught to help him understand my commands and what I want him to do. There's give-and-take on both sides, which is always a challenge since I don't know from day to day exactly how Champ will be feeling physically and mentally.

My relationship with Champ is very special, and it's constantly developing and changing. My love for my horse has definitely grown in the four years I've owned him — sounds like the kind of relationship we'd all like to have in a human partner!"

IT DOESN'T COST MUCH for you to outfit yourself for riding lessons; many of you already have most or all of what you need in your closets. Those of us who spend a lot of money on clothes for riding probably don't need much of the gear we buy; we just like to buy riding attire. In this chapter, you'll learn about the essentials and the extras.

Clothing designed especially for riding is available in your local tack shops and through catalogs, some of which are listed in the resource list at the back of this book. I've also listed a few nonriding catalogs that sell clothing you can use for riding.

Riding Essentials

Your goal should be to find riding clothes that enable you to enjoy the sport safely and comfortably.

Protective Helmets

Investing in a good riding helmet is essential. You'll be reminded about the importance of a helmet throughout this book and in many others, but here you're going to learn exactly why and how wearing a helmet can greatly minimize or eliminate the risk of one of the most serious injuries a rider can sustain — a head injury.

Horseman and physician David McLain elaborates on something we all know: When you're on a horse, you are more than 4 feet from the ground. What you may not realize is this: A headfirst fall onto a hard surface from a height of 4 feet is at the fatal threshold. In addition, a rider who falls from a horse can easily land in a headfirst position. Other factors that can contribute to the severity of a fall are the speed at which the rider is traveling — the greater the speed, the harder the impact — and the general unpredictability of horses.

"Now consider Newton's laws of motion," McLain says. "A body in motion tends to stay in motion. If you aren't wearing a helmet and you take a spill and your head hits the ground, your head stops, but the brain keeps moving, striking the skull. The impact causes damage to the brain, which can result in death or a permanent brain injury."

Considering all this, it's obvious that wearing just any old helmet won't do. A helmet not designed specifically for horseback riding will provide only minimal protection. To protect yourself fully, your helmet should meet the criteria established by the American Standard for Testing Materials (ASTM) and be approved by the Safety Equipment Institute (SEI). These helmets are labeled ASTM/SEI. (Many English barns require that you wear an approved helmet. Some, but probably most, Western barns do not, even though injury prevention experts wish they would.)

Approved helmets are made of expanded polystyrene, which crushes on impact. When the helmet hits the ground, the head keeps moving and crushes the Styrofoam lining, which absorbs energy. The helmet cushions the blow. With a helmet, according to McLain, "the rider sustains a lesser injury, or no injury at all. A helmet is cheap insurance."

Deborah Reed, Ph.D., an experienced Western rider who studies injury prevention at the University of Kentucky, notes, "Helmets with the ASTM/SEI label have undergone rigorous testing and must be able to withstand a triple gravity, or 3 g's, of impact."

These helmets also are designed to protect the areas of the head that are most vulnerable in riders; they cover a larger area of the head than a bicycle helmet, which has a more shallow design.

Tack shop owners say there are still quite a number of riding helmets being used by riders and for sale in stores that do not meet the ASTM standards. There also are helmets that aren't intended as protective headgear; they are for show only, such as the classic dressage top hat and some of the hunt caps. So when you shop for a helmet in a store or catalog, be sure to look for ASTM/SEI approval. Ask for the latest model, because efforts are constantly under way to improve them.

Consider the Weight

When you're shopping, consider the weight of the helmet. A helmet weighing only 11.5 ounces seems significantly lighter than one weighing just an ounce or two more. Many lightweight helmets with the ASTM/SEI label are vented, which really does keep your head cooler when riding on a hot day.

Western Helmets

Most riding helmets are considered "English-style," and some Western riders wear these. However, a Western-style riding helmet is now available — it's basically a helmet with a Western straw hat on top. You can buy it or order it through tack shops or from some catalogs.

Deborah Reed says the Western helmet "really is lightweight. I did some barrel racing at a rodeo recently, and not one of the rodeo riders I was with realized it was a helmet until I showed it to them. The only give-away is the chin harness." Unfortunately, many Western riders refuse to wear helmets; they are taking an unnecessary risk for head injury.

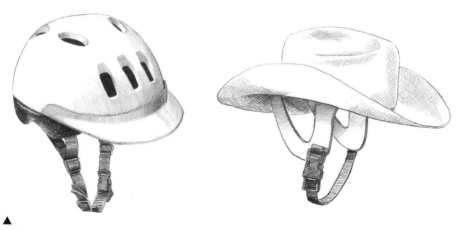

▲
Either an English-style helmet (left) or a Western-style riding helmet (right) will help protect your head if you fall.

Boots

There are two main considerations when selecting boots for riding. You want boots that will protect your feet in case a horse steps on you, and the boots should have a heel, which will prevent your foot from slipping too far through the stirrup.

The sole of your boot can have some grip, but it shouldn't be so rough that it sticks to the stirrup pad — that rubber thing in an English stirrup — or that resists coming loose if you take a spill. Occasionally, boots don't move in and out of the stirrups easily; in this case, remove the rubber stirrup pads.

You may have in your closet a solid pair of boots with a good heel that will be just fine for riding. If you need to buy a pair, though, there are many choices. Paddock boots are short boots that come just above the ankle and usually lace up. These vary widely in price. There are also sneakers designed just for riding.

The tall riding boots that many English riders favor tend to cost more than paddock boots. Tall boots are great on the trail, because they protect your legs from sharp branches and briers and provide a handy place to park your crop until you need it as you ride. The sizes available are far more varied than they used to be, and there are several calf widths. However, riders with larger calves who also are short from the knee to the heel may find that the boots in stock are too tall and come above their knees, making it nearly impossible to bend their legs. I had this problem, but with some persistence, I finally found a pair of boots that fit. Another option is to buy boots that fit your foot and leg, and have any excess height cut off by a cobbler.

If you want tall riding boots, but just can't afford those designed for riding or can't find any that fit, try to find in your local discount shoe store a pair of tall black leather "fashion" boots *modeled* after riding boots. (They may not hold up as well as a pair of boots made specifically for riding.)

You also could buy a pair of short boots, and half-chaps to fit over them. Half-chaps are made of leather or suede and cover you from ankles to knees. You zip them up to keep them on. The combination of half-chaps and short boots can look quite nice.

My favorite footwear for riding and working around the barn is a pair of construction boots I bought at the local surplus store. They aren't pretty, but they're sturdy. The two times my Draft Cross accidentally tromped me with one of his huge feet, the boots provided good protection from injury. The boots also have held up well walking through mud and muck. If you opt for construction boots, however, be sure that the soles aren't too deeply grooved and grippy (or remove those stirrup pads).

Some construction boots and boots designed for riding are available with steel toes, but a number of riders advise against them; the concern is that if you are stepped on by a horse, the steel might injure your toes even more than the horse would.

▲
Here are two popular types of riding boots.

▲
Half chaps look smart and are a good alternative to tall riding boots.

If it turns out that you will be around the barn a lot, keep a pair of rubber boots, "duck" boots, or vinyl field boots handy for rainy weather and for muddy conditions.

Of course, you can also try to find a pair of used boots. Your local tack shop may have a used or consignment clothing section, and some tack shops specialize in used riding gear.

Riding Extras

You probably don't need to invest in some of the special riding items reviewed in this section, at least initially, but once you begin riding regularly, they will make you more comfortable. Other items discussed, such as jumping vests, may not be essential when you first begin lessons but may become so as your riding skills advance.

▲
The rider on the left is wearing riding tights; the one on the right, breeches.

Riding Pants

Not long ago there was a new adult rider at the barn where I ride who was obviously fit and trim but complained that she was having trouble getting up onto the horse. The problem was her pants. She had on stiff, tight jeans and couldn't bend her knees. Pants made of stretchy material make it much easier to mount a horse. That's important for any rider, but especially for those of us who aren't as flexible as we used to be.

If you're on a budget and you're riding English, leggings work well. They fit snugly against the skin, which will prevent rubbing when you're riding English and you're going to post to the trot. Leggings aren't sold in stores as widely as they were a few years ago when they were a fashion craze, but they are plentiful in several catalogs. I've listed some that sell them in the resource section of the book.

As you begin riding English-style routinely, however, you'll want to invest in some pants designed for riding. These have patches on the inside of the calves; this is the part of your leg you'll be using for riding, and without the patches, your pants will wear out fast.

Consider opting first for a pair of riding tights. These are like a heavy-weight pair of leggings with knee patches. Riding tights generally have an elastic waist, and you pull them on. They are very stretchy and come in a variety of colors and designs. A pair that fits well will be the most comfortable piece of clothing in your closet.

You can also buy breeches or jodhpurs. Compared with casual leggings or riding tights, breeches and jodhpurs are more substantial and formal — like good slacks but made of stretchy material. In my area, breeches seem to be a more common choice than jodhpurs; they end above the ankle and are designed to be worn with high riding boots. Jodhpurs end below the ankle and are meant to be worn with short boots, although I don't think the fashion police will come after you if you wear short boots with your breeches. Both breeches and jodhpurs have patches to provide that extra coverage on your calves, and both generally close with a zipper.

Be sure to read the directions for cleaning before you buy breeches; a good number of them — often the higher-priced ones — must be dry-cleaned or hand-washed, which is reason for disqualification from my wardrobe. Also avoid buying "full-seat" breeches for now. These are riding pants with material that can grip the seat; this can pose a problem when learning to ride. They also are more costly than breeches that don't have a full seat.

Consider the color of any pants you buy for riding. Lighter colors obviously show dirt more than dark colors do, and it's hard to stay clean around a barn. If you are concerned about your appearance in riding clothes, dark colors are slimming. If you are planning to compete, beige, gray, or khaki color breeches are more appropriate show colors. If you become a serious competitor, you may have a separate wardrobe of show clothing that is not used every day.

Finding Breeches for the Hard-to-Fit

Women with a smaller waist or whose waist is small compared to their hips and thighs may find that it's hard to find breeches that fit. Those that are large enough for the thighs and seat may be too big in the waist. If you encounter this problem, try riding tights.

For men riding English, breeches are available, from catalogs and specialty stores, in regular and long lengths.

If you can't find something appropriate at your local tack shop, see the resource section at the back of the book for some mail-order options.

Western riders generally wear jeans, and no matter what style you ride, jeans are nice to wear on the trail because they are less likely to tear when you run into briers. Many of us have ruined more than one good pair of riding tights in the woods. My favorite jeans for riding are those that contain some sort of stretchy material in them, such as spandex.

Do avoid jeans that have a heavy seam down the inner legs, which might rub and irritate your skin. Some companies (e.g., Wrangler) make jeans with flat seams down the inner leg to prevent rubbing. Tack shops and catalogs also sell jeans designed for riding that have no or a minimal inner leg seam and that also have knee patches. I've heard that out West, some cowboys and cowgirls wear panty hose under their jeans to keep seams from rubbing. It might be worth a try if you want to wear the jeans you have and the seams irritate your skin.

Also avoid jeans that are very baggy, because they can lead to rubbing and sore places in your crotch — saddle sores — and on your legs.

The bottoms of jeans should fit snugly over your boots or under the top of your boots, otherwise they will ride up, exposing your lower leg to chafing. The excess material in jeans with wide bottoms also could get caught on something. Jeans with a stirrup bottom are great for riding but are difficult to find.

Stay away from any type of pants that are made of shiny slick material. You might slide right out of the saddle.

Tops

You can wear just about any blouse, T-shirt, or knit top that's comfortable, but stay away from shirts that are very long or baggy. Worn over your pants, they make it hard for your instructor to see what you're doing with your seat and hips while riding. Worn tucked in, they tend to leave big lumps of material under close-fitting riding pants.

Also select tops that can't get caught on something. I once made the mistake of wearing a loose, scooped-neck shell top on a trail ride; a branch got caught in the material in the back and I nearly got pulled off my horse before I realized what was happening.

Long sleeves are preferable for trail riding; they will protect your arms from bug bites and bramble scratches.

Underwear

The wrong underwear leads to one miserable ride! If they are too loose or too tight, they may rub, causing saddle sores. Or, they may ride up in uncomfortable ways that are difficult to correct while you're on a horse.

Men may find briefs more comfortable than boxer shorts, which might rub.

For women, briefs — full-cut underwear that go up to the waist — will give your derriere a smoother look. The top line of bikinis or hipsters usually shows through the stretchy material of tight riding pants, leaving a lump or line across your backside.

If your underwear is rubbing, try a different style. A friend of mine found that the elastic edging in regular full-cut briefs rubbed; her solution was a skimpy pair of bikinis.

People who are thin sometimes find that riding makes their seat bones sore. You can buy padded underwear from many catalogs that sell riding clothes. Initially, you may feel like you have a diaper on, but students who wear them say they do become more comfortable.

For large-breasted women, regular bras may not provide the support required during riding; you'll be bouncing around a lot, especially as you learn to trot. It may be necessary to buy a sports bra. Small-breasted women might want to try "day bras" or "cami" bras, which are bras that slip over the head and have no metal fasteners. They are comfortable for riding and less expensive than a sports bra.

Outerwear

As with tops, for riding select coats with a design that doesn't obscure the instructor's view of your seat. Nor do you want a coat or jacket that will bunch up under your seat on the saddle. Thus, a waist-length jacket may be best. There also are riding jackets that come below the waist but taper at the bottom; these won't obstruct the view of your riding position as much as an untapered jacket would, and won't get caught under your seat.

Try to wear outerwear with pockets. When you're on a horse, you don't want to have to get off to fetch a tissue or a pair of gloves.

A vinyl poncho or rain slicker isn't a necessity, but it's nice to have on hand when you're caught around the barn in rainy weather.

Selecting Safe Outerwear

Don't forget safety when selecting outerwear. Steer clear of coats, jackets, and sweatshirts that have pull strings, which can catch easily in the horse's bridle or reins or on objects around the barn.

Gloves

In winter, gloves for riding will be necessary to keep warm. Gloves also may be important on very hot summer days: If your hands sweat, it's hard to hold onto the reins without gloves. Some riders wear gloves year-round to protect their hands and nails and to avoid calluses.

In choosing gloves for riding, be sure to select a pair with palms that grip well so the reins don't slide through your hands, and gloves that are snug enough that they won't come off easily while you're riding. You don't have to buy gloves specifically designed for riding, although plenty are available. A thin pair of gloves with palms that grip will work just fine.

Protective Vests

Protective vests are a newer type of gear on the riding scene. They are designed to minimize impact on the torso in the event of a fall. Some of them also cover your shoulders. The barn where I ride was the first in my area to require students who jump to wear a protective vest; other barns are now following suit.

These vests are expensive. But if you are planning to learn how to jump, or you are going to be learning a high-speed type of riding activity, a protective vest might be something to consider, whether or not your stable requires you to wear one. If the price of this product is out of your reach, you could split the cost and share the vest with a riding friend who would wear the same size.

▲
Wearing a protective vest is a good idea when you're jumping.

Socks

Why would anyone need advice about the socks you wear for riding? Because if you don't select them carefully, you'll find they inch down under your heel, which is really aggravating when it happens in the middle of a ride. You don't want to have to get off your horse to fix a bunched-up sock. I've found that the socks designed for boots, called boot socks, are the most likely to stay put. These generally are tall socks that cover the calf, and are made of snug, stretchy material. Catalogs for riders sell them, as do some boot stores.

Beware of any sock that has thick seams around the toe. They can rub. Try to find socks with stretchy material that's smooth from toe to top.

Dressing for Weather Extremes

Riding in very hot or cold weather can be a miserable experience if you're dressed inappropriately. If you plan ahead, you'll be comfortable.

Hot Weather

In hot weather, try to ride during the cooler times of day. Wear the lightest shirt you can, and wear lightweight pants.

Soak a bandanna in cold water and tie it around your neck. You could also purchase a "cooling" bandanna — a bandanna that absorbs and retains water — to wear inside your helmet to keep your head cool. These products are available in tack shops and from most equestrian catalogs. A thin sweatband around your forehead will prevent sweat from dripping into your eyes, which can really sting. If it's scorching hot outside, you might even want to soak your head in water before putting on your helmet.

Have plenty of cool water on hand. Fill plastic containers halfway with water, then freeze. Before you go to ride, fill the rest of the container with tap water and toss the bottle in the car. The frozen half usually keeps the water cold for several hours. You can use store-bought containers, or save plastic soda bottles of any size for this purpose. Take smaller bottles in a saddle pad for a trail ride on a hot day. Or keep a larger bottle by the riding ring during your lesson; most instructors will encourage you to drink and will be happy to hand you your bottle when you need a swig.

If you really get overheated, soak yourself with the hose after your ride.

Besides coping with the heat, pesky gnats, flies, and bees are another common problem if you're around a barn in hot weather, so keep bug repellent handy.

Again, it's a good idea to wear riding gloves on a scorching-hot day to prevent sweaty palms from impairing your grip on the reins.

And don't forget the sunscreen!

Cold Weather

In very cold weather, layered clothing is imperative. Once you warm up in a riding class, you'll probably need to remove an outer layer. Be sure to let your instructor know that you want to remove clothing so she can hold your horse (or ask you to dismount, if necessary); some horses become frightened when they see a piece of clothing flapping around their back.

For the bottom half of winter attire, many riders prefer to layer first with silk long underwear, although I've found that a pair of panty hose, tights, or leggings works well. Cover these with the heaviest pants you have that are comfortable for riding. Or you can buy a pair of riding pants lined with material such as polar fleece, which is designed to keep you warm.

For your top half, wear a silk undershirt or a traditional thermal undershirt. I can't tolerate wool against my skin, so I cover my cotton thermal undershirt with one (and sometimes two) cotton, long-sleeved turtlenecks, then put on a wool sweater and top it off with my winter riding jacket. You'll want a jacket that is insulated for cold weather.

There are headbands and earmuffs designed to wear with riding helmets; these are a good investment, because keeping your head warm keeps you warmer overall. Polar fleece neck warmers, which keep cold air off your neck, also are great. If the temperatures are so cold that your face is susceptible to frostbite, you can pull up neck warmers over your cheeks and nose.

To keep your hands warm, buy a pair of glove liners and cover them with a pair of winter gloves with a palm that grips. Silk glove liners are inexpensive and they're thin, which is a necessity as you must be able to grasp the reins.

Do invest in one or two pairs of good socks made of material designed to keep you warm in winter, or in good wool socks. These cost just a bit more than boot socks. You should be able to move your toes in your boots. If you can't, your toes really will freeze.

Boots for Bitter Weather

Unlined leather riding boots or shoes aren't likely to keep your toes warm enough in bitter winter weather, and you may find that boots specifically for winter riding are a necessity. These are made of modern materials designed to keep you warm.

You'll find that once you are moving on the horse, the horse helps keep your legs warm and the exercise warms the rest of you. You are more likely to suffer from the cold while you are in the barn, grooming the horse. The best protection I've found against a freezing-cold, damp barn is a pair of traditional ski bibs, which I wear over riding clothing. They are bulky and too slick to wear to ride but you can slip them off easily for riding and slip them on again after a ride, as necessary.

4 Injury Prevention and Riding Safety

Patricia Bass works full time and she's a mom, too. She took up riding at the age of 37. She also ultimately bought her own horse and rides two or three times weekly.

"When I ride, there's a passage for communication between my horse and me. Therefore, the better rider I am, the better the communication. Whether I have a good ride or a poor one, afterward I always feel exhilarated, less stressed, and have a sense that I accomplished something. The muscle aches, flies, and dirt just go with the territory."

A SURVEY CONDUCTED by the Horse Industry Alliance concludes that perceived risk is one of the major reasons that people who want to take up riding don't.

Statistics on riding injuries can be scary. In 1995, for instance, the National Electronic Surveillance System reported more than 65,000 hospital emergency room admissions for horse-related injuries. But these statistics may give a skewed picture of the risk to those who ride safe horses, have safe instructors, and ride in a safe environment. Throughout this chapter you'll learn more about how to stay safe and minimize the risk of the minor stresses and strains that can occur from riding and working with horses.

Reducing the Risk

According to instructor Paul Novograd, injuries happen in unstructured situations, when novices are put onto horses they can't handle in less than ideal situations. At a lesson barn with good instructors and safe horses, "the risk for injury is actually quite small," he says.

Lari Shea, of Ricochet Ridge Ranch in Fort Bragg, California, takes hundreds of adults annually on recreational rides along beaches and on trails in California, and many of these riders have never been on a horse before. The first instruction they get is from Shea, so she has plenty of experience with novice riders.

"There's a distinct element of risk in horseback riding," she says. "But once you have people riding safe horses and wearing protective headgear, the rate of serious injury plummets. In fact, the norm is for no one to get hurt. We've never had one serious injury on my ranch in 25 years. I'm not saying it couldn't happen, but in a well-run riding program, it's unlikely."

Former instructor David Butts notes, "That doesn't mean you won't ever fall off and feel bad a day or two. But you'll heal like anyone else. If you're an average adult in generally good health, the risk for injury while riding is more perceived than real."

David McLain, a rheumatologist, rider, and safety committee chairman for the United States Combined Training Association (USCTA), points out that about 60 percent of horseback riding accidents happen at home — among people riding outside of a lesson program or a controlled situation. "In our studies of riding injuries in the USCTA-recognized events," he says, "including higher-level riding activities such as cross-country and stadium jumping as well as steeplechasing, we found a low 0.37 percent injury rate per competitor." The catastrophic riding injury suffered by actor Christopher Reeve in 1995, which resulted in permanent paralysis, grabbed national headlines, but it really was a freak accident, according to McLain.

In McLain's opinion, riding is a safe sport if you: (1) learn how to ride safey; (2) wear proper equipment, including a state-of-the-art riding helmet; (3) ride a horse you can handle; and (4) ride at your level and don't try riding beyond your capabilities.

My experience also substantiates that riding is a safe sport. Over the past decade, I've ridden with a lot of other average adult pleasure riders. I can honestly say that I can't think of one of us who has sustained a serious injury riding in a safe, controlled lesson program. Most of us have taken a tumble now and then, usually when we were out in the woods riding on our own outside of a lesson, but because we ride safe horses and we ride safely, in all instances these mishaps resulted in no more than minor scrapes and bruises, and often a good laugh or two.

The bottom line is that riding does involve some risk and freak accidents do occur. But it's also true that if you ride a safe horse in a good lesson program or supervised outing, and if you wear your protective helmet, it's unlikely that you'll be seriously injured while riding.

Coping with Fear

If getting onto a large animal gives you butterflies, you're not alone. Instructors agree that new adult riders are more fearful than children who take up riding. With age, we're more aware that life involves risk and that bad things can happen to any of us. But keep the risks that come with horseback riding in perspective.

"Fear is a normal response," says Lari Shea. "There's nothing natural about humans getting onto the back of a horse. It's normal to feel out of your element and uncomfortable, both physically and emotionally," when riding for the first time.

If you want to ride but are fearful, discuss it with your instructor. If your instructor doesn't take your concerns seriously, find an instructor who does. A sensitive instructor is likely to be especially careful to assign a docile horse. She may have to lead you around on the horse for the first lesson, or even the first several. "With time and the right instructor," Shea promises, "that fear will lessen."

Paul Novograd, of Claremont Riding Academy in New York, believes there is one type of fear that perhaps should discourage an adult from taking up riding. It's the kind of fear that makes you so scared that you are extremely tense and rigid in the saddle. Riding requires following the motion of the horse, and when you're overly tense and can't relax, that can actually predispose you to falls and injury. The driving motivation for these students isn't so much a love of horses or a desire to learn to ride, says Novograd, but conquering fear. "If you're so frightened that you're constantly riding with your heart in your mouth, perhaps another sport would be a better option," he says.

If you want to ride but are seriously concerned about your safety, you might want to stick to riding in an English saddle. Deborah Reed, Ph.D., an assistant professor at the University of Kentucky who studies injury and is herself an accomplished rider, says, "You're more likely to get hurt coming out of a Western saddle. If you [collide with] a Western saddle horn, painful bruising and fractures are very likely to occur."

David Butts, also an experienced rider and horse trainer, says that English saddles are safer because you're less likely to get hung up if you take a tumble: "I've been hurt coming out of a Western saddle, but never coming out of an English," he says.

Safe Ground Procedures

Many people assume they are most vulnerable to injury while riding, but according to Deborah Reed, that's not necessarily the case: "People always equate speed and height with injury on a horse, and it's true — you could sustain more serious injuries if you fall off at high speeds, or if you are jumping higher, because the impact will be greater. But these aren't the only ways you can get hurt around horses."

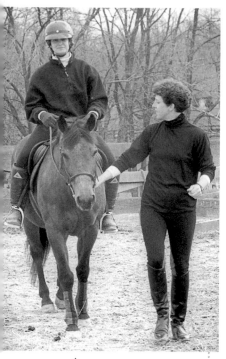

▲
If you are afraid of riding, find an instructor who will be sensitive to your fears and help build your confidence.

There's also the risk of injury from horses while you're on the ground. If you are working in a confined environment, like a stall, "you could get banged against a wall," Reed cautions. In fact, her work indicates that ground injuries while working with horses, especially mares and foals, may be more common than injuries while riding.

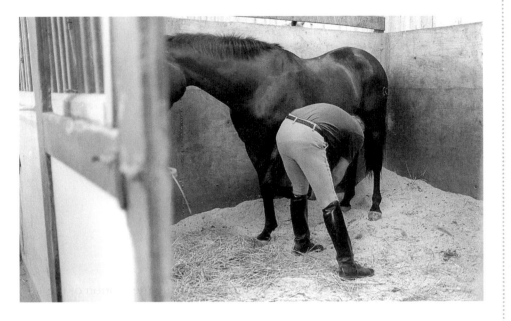

◀

To stay safe around horses, be just as careful working with them on the ground as you are while you're riding. This rider has wisely positioned herself so she can get out through the stall door quickly if need be.

10 Tips for Ground Safety

Always remember that horses are large animals, weighing on average 1,000 pounds. Common sense will help you work with them safely on the ground. Here are some tips to get you started:

1. **Read about it.** To stay safe around horses, learn all you can about handling yourself around horses and about horse behavior. (See the recommended readings at the back of the book for an annotated list of my favorite publications on horses and horse safety.) Certainly, reading about horses is not the same as handling them, but the more you know, the more confident and comfortable you'll be.

2. **Wear a helmet.** One of the most important things you can do to protect yourself is to wear an ASTM/SEI-labeled riding helmet while working on the ground around horses. (See chapter 3 for more on helmets.)

3. **Avoid horses that are showing signs of irritation or upset.** When a horse is irritated, upset, or in a grumpy mood, he'll tell you by laying back his ears, waving his head at you, baring his teeth, or turning his rump toward you when you enter the stall. You need to learn to read these signs. *Never* approach a horse exhibiting this kind of behavior. Get an instructor or someone else with experience to help you.

4. **Learn how to approach a horse.** Use a normal tone of voice when approaching a horse — don't whisper or yell. Approach the horse from an angle, in a calm, confident manner, moving toward the horse's

shoulder. If you approach directly from behind or in front, the horse may not be able to see you and you could make him nervous or startle him.

5. **Give yourself an out.** When working around horses, while grooming, for example, you always want to give yourself an out, preferably on more than one side, so you can move away quickly if a horse starts to act up. The barn where you'll be taking lessons should have grooming areas set up with your safety in mind. If you're in the stall, leave the stall door open and position yourself so you can exit quickly.

6. **Never walk behind a horse.** Despite this general rule, you'll often notice people in barns walking behind horses. Usually it's because they know the horses and are pretty confident that they won't get kicked. If they are experienced, you'll also notice that when they do walk behind a horse, they stick close to the rump; if something unexpectedly upsets the usually calm animal and causes him to kick out, there's less impact than there would be standing 2 feet behind him, because at 2 feet away and with fuller extension of the leg, he can strike harder. They also keep one hand or their arm on the horse to let the horse know they are there. When they are grooming the tail, they stand to the side of the horse's rump.

In short, never walk behind a horse if you don't know him well enough to be reasonably certain he won't kick out, and if you do walk behind him, follow the close-to-the-rump method. Stand to the side when grooming around the rear end. If you have to walk behind a horse you aren't tending, allow yourself about 12 feet of clearance.

7. **Learn safe leading procedures.** You always need to keep control of the horse's head. One way to do that is by holding the reins or the lead rope several inches under the horse's chin, and by walking next to the front of the horse's shoulder, not in front of him, where you can't see him and observe his reaction to everything.

Do be sure to use a lead rope when you're leading a horse with a halter. You'll have a lot more control; if you only hang onto the halter, the horse can easily get away. Don't loop a lead rope (or the reins) around your hand or arms — you could get caught and dragged if something scares the horse and he takes off.

8. **Keep your horse away from other horses.** While leading a horse, keep him away from other horses to ensure that they don't get into a scuffle. If they do, it's really easy to get slammed against a wall or to get your foot stepped on.

Don't lead a horse too close to stalled horses with their heads sticking out. If you have to pass another horse in the aisle of the barn, ask the person tending that horse if it's okay. Usually, that person will offer to move the horse aside to give you plenty of safe passing room. If not, ask him to move the horse to give you more room. *Good communication among people at a barn goes a long way in preventing accidents.*

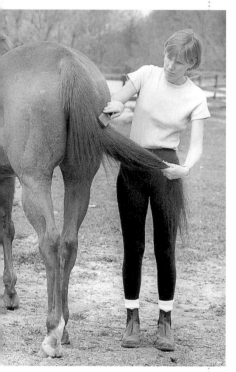

▲
When grooming a horse's tail, stand to the side, not directly behind the animal.

9. **Restrain horses safely.** Some horses are trained to stand in cross ties for grooming and some aren't; they are accustomed to being tied to a post. The cross ties that attach to the horse's halter should have "panic snaps" that can be detached easily if the horse panics. When a horse is in cross ties, it's also a good idea to use a safety or breakaway halter, which should break if he panics and rears, and to attach the ends of the cross ties to baling twine, which also will break. A horse tied to a post should be secured with a quick-release knot. Learn to work defensively: Always have a way out, and always keep an eye on the horse you are handling.

Before grooming a horse, be sure to ask where you should groom and exactly how you should restrain him.

▲
Here's a horse in cross ties with panic snaps attached to the halter. If the horse panics, the snaps come quickly undone.

How to Tie a Quick-Release Knot

a. Fold the rope to make a loop about 8 inches long and leaving about 6 inches of the end free. Pass the loop through the tie ring.

b. Now twist the rope several times, leaving a small bit of open loop at the end.

c. Pass a short loop of the section of rope that leads back to your horse through the loop at the base of the twist.

d. Now pass a short loop of the *end section* through the second (horse-end) loop, pull on the horse-end of the rope, and draw the whole knot snug.

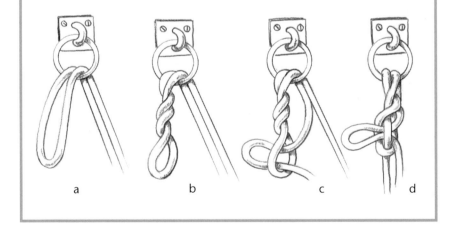

a   b   c   d

---

10. **Take care in the pasture.** Horses should be trained not to take off the minute you walk them through a gate into a pasture. The proper method is to walk a horse through the gate, close the gate almost all the way to block the horse, and then turn the horse toward you before releasing the lead rope (and removing the halter if it's to be removed).

Before turning out a horse into a pasture, make sure the horse is well behaved and not in the habit of taking off. Ask someone with experience to go with you the first few times. *Always* ask someone with experience to accompany you if you are turning one horse out into a pasture full of horses. You may need someone to shoo horses away from the gate while you turn your horse out.

Also ask someone with experience to come along if you have to take your horse *through* a pasture of horses to get to another pasture or to get him out of a pasture. If the horses in the pasture start to run around you or try to play with the horse you're leading, you may need help shooing them away. Carry a whip to wave away any horse that tries to approach. Try to follow the fence line so that if a stampede occurs, you can let go of the horse you're leading and escape over the fence!

"Treat" Safety

Never, ever walk into a pasture with horses while carrying hay, carrots, or anything else they can eat. You could find yourself in the middle of a major scuffle.

Safety While Riding

Never ride a horse you can't handle. It's that simple. Reputable, experienced instructors are unanimous in their advice that new adult riders should ride quiet horses. You may *think* you want to ride a frisky horse, but don't if you're serious about staying safe.

"Temperament has everything to do with it," says Deborah Reed. "Ride a settled, older horse, preferably a gelding." She also recommends that you stick to things the horse knows. For instance, when on a horse that you know is used for trail riding, don't try a jump unless your instructor or the barn owner tells you the horse knows how to jump and that it's okay. If you're riding a horse that's used primarily in the ring, don't assume that he is calm on the trail. Ask.

When you're new at riding, it can be hard to tell if you're "outhorsing" yourself or what you should ask each horse to do. That's why you've got to select a lesson barn wisely, as discussed in the previous chapter, and put some faith in your instructor.

If you are tempted to ride other than at your carefully chosen lesson barn, proceed cautiously and don't assume that every barn practices safe riding. Ask around first to determine which stables are recommended as fun but safe places to ride. When you're out of town, perhaps the hotel staff where you're staying can make recommendations; or you could make a few calls to local tack shops. A good riding facility will carefully question you about your riding experience, then assign an appropriate horse.

Once you've ridden awhile, you'll readily learn to tell whether you're on a horse that's too much for you. Some horses are sensitive to the rider's legs; if you barely touch them, they move on out. This is a risk because beginning riders haven't yet learned to control their legs well and will tend to grip, which will only make this kind of horse go faster. A horse that doesn't stop readily when asked to is a risk. If you feel like you're sitting on a time bomb and you're frightened, get off, ask for a quieter horse, and don't feel you need to apologize.

Authorities agree that riders also are more likely to be injured while learning a new skill, such as cantering; when trying to teach the horse a new skill; or while riding over rough terrain. Don't take on new skills or ride on different, especially rough, terrain unless you and your instructor think you're ready. And when you first try a new skill or riding area, do so with supervision.

Ring Safety

Staying safe while riding in the ring requires good manners. Manners also keep your fellow riders from getting angry at you. The rules at various barns may vary, so check them out and follow them to the letter. Some common rules that may be posted at your lesson barn include:

1. **Pass left to left.** This means that if someone is coming the opposite way, the horses pass left shoulder to left shoulder. It's really just like driving your car on the right side of the road — you pass driver door to driver door.

◀
Riders should pass left to left. Following this basic rule helps prevent collisions.

2. **Riders proceeding at the faster pace have the right-of-way on the track.** If several people are cantering or trotting around the track and you want to walk, you should walk inside the track, not on the track, which blocks the pace of the others.

3. **Announce yourself when entering and leaving an indoor arena.** This is an important rule, whether you are leading a horse or just walking alone. When you enter the arena, say something like, "Door!" or "Coming in the door!" This prevents you from spooking any horses being worked in the ring or any horses being led out of the ring.
4. **Majority rules.** When most of the people in the ring are jumping, for example, you can't come in and walk your horse around the ring if you'll be in the way.

Ring Etiquette

There are several other rules that everyone should follow but that often aren't posted. They involve the kind of riding behavior that can threaten the safety of others, but more often simply gets on people's nerves. Some riders just haven't yet learned to ride and control their horse well enough to stay out of everyone else's way, or they aren't aware that their riding behavior is intrusive. To help keep the riding experience pleasant and safe for you and your riding partners, I recommend the following:

- **Don't tailgate.** Riding on someone else's tail can be really disconcerting to the rider getting tailgated, especially if it causes his or her horse to act up. In general, stay away from other horses — leave at least one horse length between you and another rider unless your instructor tells you otherwise.

- **Allow ample room when passing and crossing.** When passing the horse in front of you, allow plenty of clearance — at least the width of a couple of horses — as you pull out and around. Get well in front of the horse — again at least a couple of horse lengths — before moving back onto the track.

  When you cut across a ring, as you will learn to do to keep a proper distance from other horses, don't cut back in front of another horse and rider. Again, allow at least two horse lengths.

- **Don't stop dead in your tracks.** Unless you've got an emergency, avoid stopping dead in your tracks when other riders are behind you. Pull off the track if you have to halt; it's better than causing the riders behind you to pile up, which interrupts the flow of the class and interferes with your fellow students' riding.

- **Be quick to apologize.** Despite your best efforts, your horse may occasionally stop and cause a pileup, or you may mean to provide more clearance when passing but miscalculate and cut someone off. Apologize to the other rider or riders as appropriate; just showing you mean to be courteous goes a long way toward keeping the riding experience pleasant for everyone.

Trail Safety

You've got to be even more on guard riding on the trail than in a ring because you're more likely to encounter the unexpected. It might be a rabbit hopping across the path, a herd of deer leaping by, or a plastic bag blowing around on a branch.

When you're riding out with instructors or guides, as you should be when you're a beginning rider, they will set the rules and control the ride. But when you start to ride out onto the trail with friends, you'll all need to take responsibility for ensuring the safety of yourselves and each other. Here's how the group I ride with does it, and we've managed to trail ride for many years without serious incident.

1. **Agree on the level of the ride.** If you want to walk on the trail and aren't yet prepared to trot and canter along, don't ride out with more advanced people who like to hotdog it. You'll either hold them back or, worse, have to go faster than you want and be uncomfortable.

   Conversely, if you want to ride at a brisk pace, don't invite people along who don't like to ride at faster gaits without clarifying your plans; either explain that you're going out for a brisk ride, so they can decline, or agree to ride at the slower pace the lower-level riders can comfortably handle.

2. **Ride in groups.** When riding within about one-half mile of the barn, you can probably ride with just one other; one of you could summon help quickly if need be by riding back to the barn. But three riders is better, and should be the minimum if you are riding farther out. That way, there's one person to stay with a person who is injured and the third could go for help.

3. **Appoint a leader.** Before riding out, agree which horse and rider will lead. The horse that leads should be the one that's the least likely to spook. Some horses prefer to lead; others would rather follow.

   If you all have horses that are pretty bomb-proof and can ride in any position in the line, you might want to take turns leading. My group often does this because we want our horses to stay accustomed to being in any position in the line.

4. **Stay properly spaced.** Don't get too far ahead of the riders behind you so that their horses don't unexpectedly decide to go fast and catch up; don't get too far behind the riders in front of you so your horse doesn't do the same thing.

5. **Announce gait changes.** Especially if you are the leader, inform the other riders before you pick up a trot or canter or before you change from a faster gait to a walk or halt. If you don't, they might not be prepared for the change in gait, and could take a spill if caught unaware.

6. **Alert other riders to hazards.** When you see a herd of deer moving through the woods, notice hikers approaching — or anything else that might cause a horse to shy or spook — warn your fellow riders so they can prepare.

   One hazard we've found is hikers in the woods who think they are supposed to hide behind a tree and not say a word because horses are approaching. They mean well, but the horses aren't sure what's up ahead and really get antsy. We handle this problem by politely saying something like, "Hello! Please go ahead and speak so the horses know you're a person!" That usually gets the message across.

7. **Stay on the bridle path.** Where I live, we're losing trails rapidly to development, so we're always trying to find new places to ride without tresspassing. We quickly learned that there are hazards to be found off the established bridle trail — primarily barbed wire left over from long-gone farms. It's often lying on the ground, under leaves, and impossible to see. We've also found deep holes that were masked by sticks and leaves. To prevent your horse from being injured by these hazards, always walk a trail before you ride it to make sure there are no hazards. Use surveyor's tape to mark trees as you walk a new trail so you'll be able to follow the same path again.

8. **Carry a cell phone.** Wear a fanny pack and carry a cell phone. Write down the phone number of the barn and tape it to the back of the cell phone, just in case you panic in an emergency and forget the number. (Let's hope you won't need to call 911). I'd advise against carrying the cell phone in a saddle pad pocket or saddlebag; if you get dumped and your horse takes off, it won't do you much good.

9. **Pay attention. Pay attention. Pay attention.** Almost every time my riding friends and I have had a near-incident on the trail, it's because we were gabbing away and not paying attention. Yap as much as you want, but keep your eyes peeled in the same direction that your horse is looking!

10. **If a horse is acting up, go home.** Don't push it. When you are out on a ride and one of the horses starts to act up, go back to the barn. Even a usually well-behaved horse will have a bad day and may seem spooky, especially frisky, or just on edge. If a rider is having trouble with a horse, don't push her to keep going.

    We've had newer trail riders in our group from time to time who got out onto the trail, realized they were frightened by their horse's behavior, but felt embarrassed about asking to turn back. We make it clear that there's nothing to be embarrassed about and encourage a return to the barn in good-natured fashion. It's the smart thing to do. Be sensitive to what's going on with your fellow trail riders.

11. **Protect yourself from hunters.** Trail riders must be aware of hunting season and take necessary precautions. During hunting season, don't ride in woods where hunting is permitted. Perhaps a greater danger

than riding in woods where hunting is permitted is encountering illegal hunters in woods where hunting is not allowed. The fact that they are hunting illegally implies that they aren't going to be as responsible shooting as would be someone who hunts legally. Avoid riding anywhere where there are reports of illegal hunting.

Even when you ride in woods where you don't expect to encounter hunters, protect yourself by wearing lots of bright orange during hunting season. My group wears orange hunting vests and orange ski caps on top of our riding helmets. We are fashion disasters, but you can see us coming from a good distance. We also attach sleigh bells to the D-rings on our saddles — beware: some horses don't like bells — and talk a lot while riding so that deer and hunters know we're coming through. You can also buy orange half-sheets for your horse.

Managing Stress and Strain

Perhaps more of a problem than serious injuries among horseback riders is the development of minor stresses and strains and everyday "boo-boos." These can result when you first begin to ride and use muscles you didn't know you had; from frequent riding — if you take to it, like so many of us have done; and from common chores around the barn.

Acute Aches and Pains from Riding

When you first begin riding, remember to take it easy. You may experience some minor, generalized soreness, especially in the legs. Try walking around; this may make you feel better. I've always found that a long hot shower helps. This kind of minor soreness should disappear in 24 to 48 hours (and if not, call your doctor).

You're more likely to be sore after riding if you don't warm up your muscles beforehand, so take the time to stretch before class. Reach your arms above your head; touch your toes (with knees slightly bent); twist at the waist with arms out to the side; or jog in place for a few minutes.

If you have pulled something specific — a calf muscle, for example — and there is tenderness and swelling, an easy-to-remember, widely recommended treatment is RICE:

*R*est
*I*ce
*C*ompression
*E*levation

Experts advise that if you sustain an injury, don't resume exercise until several days *after* the pain is gone. Of course, if you're not positive your injury is minor, call your physician.

Preventing Chronic Problems

In an October 1995 article in *Equus,* appropriately entitled "Ouch!," Allison Rogers says that if you ride regularly, catastrophic injury isn't the greatest concern; ". . . your greatest risks are the more subtle hazards of spending time in the saddle, the everyday aches and pains produced by pulled tendons, strained ligaments, inflamed joints, and jostled vertebrae."

If you're a lower-level pleasure rider, you might be even more prone to sprains and strains because you probably aren't as fit as a more advanced rider. You may not have the muscle strength needed to support and stabilize your joints and spine, which in turn can contribute to a wearing-down of joint cartilage. The result could be conditions such as arthritis, bursitis, and tendinitis, which can become disabling over time, according to Rogers.

The way to protect yourself from these chronic conditions, say experts, is proper fitness exercises to strengthen muscles and support your joints. You learned in chapter 1 that while riding will help you stay fit, you can't really count on riding alone to provide all the exercise you may need. Some examples of exercises that can help strengthen your body follow. Don't do them if they cause pain anywhere. Assuming you can do them, though, begin slowly — do only a few repetitions of each to begin with — then build up your stamina by doing a few more each week.

Walking Leg Lunges. Stand with feet shoulder-width apart. Take one step forward with your right leg. Bend both knees until the back, left knee is about 1 foot off the floor. As you rise, bring the back left leg forward so that it is even with your other foot. Repeat with the left leg forward.

Upper Back Exercise (Scapular Retraction). While standing, raise your arms to the side at about shoulder height. Bend your elbows 90 degrees, hands facing forward. Move your arms backward so that your elbows are coming toward each other. Hold for 5 seconds, then release.

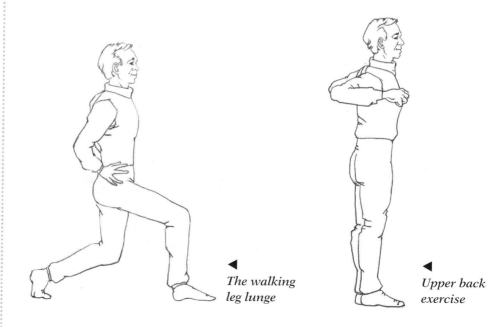

◀ *The walking leg lunge*

◀ *Upper back exercise*

Modified Push-ups. Get on the floor on your hands and knees, with your arms about shoulder-width apart. Slowly bend your elbows and touch your nose to the floor (or as nearly so as you're able), then slowly push yourself back up.

◀ *A modified push-up*

Back and Hip Exercise. Lie on your stomach and rest your forehead on your hands. Slowly lift the right leg off the floor; about 2 inches is enough. Hold for 2 seconds, then lower. Repeat on other side.

◀ *Back and hip exercise*

Many new adult riders come to class with some kind of chronic problem — a bad back seems to be the usual one, probably because it's a very common problem among the general population. If back pain is a frequent problem for you, consult your physician before you ride. Also discuss the situation with your instructor and ask if it's possible to be assigned a horse that might be easier on you. Some horses will give you a much rougher ride than others. While you are learning to ride properly, it really can help to have a smoother horse.

Health professionals point out that there are different types of back problems. If you have trouble with your back, you need to get an accurate diagnosis from your physician, who also should be able to prescribe some back-strengthening exercises appropriate for your condition.

Making Chores Easier

The chores that go along with caring for horses can be more taxing than riding if you aren't careful. Following are some of those chores that can give you a strain, and how to prevent them from leading to injury.

Cleaning Buckets. Avoid lifting full water buckets. They are really heavy. Even when half full, lifting buckets off their hooks and carrying them out can put a serious strain on your back and arms.

Instead, get an empty bucket — perhaps the horse's feed bucket — and set it on the ground under the water bucket you want to clean.

To empty buckets, tip them — don't lift.

This rider is using her thighs to support the back leg and hoof and is bending at the knees, which helps reduce strain on the back.

Tip — don't lift — the water bucket from its hook and pour at least half its contents into the empty bucket underneath. Pour in only as much water as you can comfortably carry. You may be able to carry two buckets, each partially filled with water, to balance yourself. Make a few trips to avoid straining yourself.

If there isn't a hose that reaches the bucket for refilling, reverse the procedure above to refill, using a clean bucket to haul smaller amounts of water.

Picking Out Feet. A well-behaved horse will lift and try to hold each leg up, enabling you to clean the hooves without stressing your back. You'll still have some weight to manage, though, especially with the back hooves.

Use the same approach as you would lifting a heavy box: Bend at the knees and support yourself with your legs; don't bend over with your legs straight. Place the hand nearer the horse under the hoof and rest the hoof on your thighs. Then clean out the foot with the other hand.

Be careful to move your toes away from the spot where the horse will put his foot back down. To prevent getting caught with a hoof, guide the horse's leg back down gently with your hand instead of releasing the leg while it's up in the air, which will cause the horse to slam the foot back down. Don't try to hang on to a horse that is jerking its leg away. He may be losing his balance. Let it go, and then try again. If you still have no success, ask for help before the horse learns a bad habit.

Don't get down on your knee or knees; it's tempting sometimes, but when working around horses, you always want to be ready to spring away if need be.

Lifting Hay Bales. Bales of hay can weigh a lot, so don't try to carry one. Remove the wire or string holding it together and carry a few flakes as needed, or ask for help moving the bale.

Removing Wet Bedding. A bucket full of manure and wet bedding is incredibly heavy! If you're placing soiled bedding in a bucket without wheels that needs to be moved for dumping on the manure pile, simply don't put in too much. As with the water buckets, make more trips with a lighter-weight bucket; don't try to carry one very full one. Better yet, see if the barn has a lightweight wheelbarrow that you can use to transport manure and wet bedding, and ask for help dumping it. Again, don't put too much in at once.

Carrying Tack. Lifting and toting saddles and putting them in place on high racks can be very stressful to your back. Instead of reaching way over your head to place a saddle on a rack, take the time to get a stool to make the chore easier. If you have your own saddle, see whether you can arrange to have a tack trunk near your grooming area so you don't have to carry the saddle around too much.

Barn Etiquette

Even though the rule may not be posted, many barns expect you to clean up the aisle or tack area when the horse you're grooming defecates or if you make a mess cleaning out the horse's feet. The staff at most barns just couldn't keep up with the mess unless riders cleaned up after themselves and their horses.

Wound Care

Working with horses around a barn, you're likely to sustain knicks, cuts, and scrapes and to pick up splinters. Most well-run barns have a first-aid kit on hand, but it's a good idea to keep your own supplies in the car. Even minor cuts and abrasions — anything that breaks the skin — should be treated immediately. Here's what I've found is useful in a first-aid kit:

- Antiseptic
- Antibiotic ointment
- Adhesive strips (Band-Aids)
- Tweezers

Tetanus Immunization

Make sure your tetanus shot is up-to-date. Tetanus is caused by the spore-forming bacillus *Clostridium tetani*. The clinical manifestations of tetanus include lockjaw, muscle spasm, respiratory spasm, seizures, and paralysis. Few people actually contract tetanus these days, thanks largely to immunization, but it's a real risk if you aren't immunized, and the disease is potentially fatal.

Many adults think tetanus immunization is only for kids, but adults can contract tetanus. In fact, the largest proportion of cases that still occur are in the southeastern United States, in the summer months, among adults older than 50. Virtually all cases are in people who either never were vaccinated or haven't had a booster following initial vaccination, according to information from the Centers for Disease Control and Prevention.

Tetanus is more likely to occur in puncture wounds and deep wounds that are contaminated with dirt. And what do you find around barns? Lots of dirt.

A tetanus immunization lasts about 10 years, but if you sustain a puncture wound or a cut that needs stitching and haven't had a booster in more than 5 years, you'll need a tetanus shot.

Dry, Cracked Skin

It may seem silly to devote a section to dry, cracked skin, but it's one of the most common complaints heard around a barn during wintertime. Riders and horse owners are outdoors a lot, exposing their skin to the elements, and wash their hands often — rightly so — because they get so dirty. The result is dry, cracked skin. The cracks may get so bad that they bleed, which can be especially painful.

Get into the habit of wearing gloves in cold weather, and keep an extra pair around in case the ones you have on become wet. Keep a good moisturizer in your tack box, locker, or car, and use it often. By protecting your skin and keeping it moist, you can prevent the development of painful cracks.

Some of my friends have found that when they develop cracked skin, Bag Balm, a product originally developed to treat mastitis in cows, is soothing and seems to speed the healing process. (Most tack shops and feed stores stock it.) A triple antibiotic ointment (Neosporin) is another favorite remedy.

Horse Tack and Supplies

5

A graphic artist, wife, and mother, Maggie Brodnick resumed riding at age 35. She rides twice a week, and hopes to buy her own horse soon.

"I realized that unless I took control and got over the feeling of being 'selfish' by taking up riding, I would never do something that I'd loved so much as a child. Riding brings a joy to my life that's hard to explain: the beauty of the animal; the thrill (and occasional fear) of the physical challenge; the nonverbal communication between horse and rider. It all adds up to a moment in time each week that I'll never give up."

NOW THAT YOU'RE GETTING SERIOUS about riding, and you think you may buy a horse some day, you should become familiar with the tack and other equipment and supplies necessary for horses. You might even want to start investing in some of your own.

Saddles

There are more types of saddles available today than you can count. Some students purchase a saddle even before they buy a horse so they have their own comfortable seat. Ideally, saddles should be fit to the horse, but an average saddle is likely to fit many average horses. The kind of saddle you buy should be determined by the type of riding you plan to do.

Saddles are available at tack shops and through catalogs. The downside to ordering a saddle from a catalog is that you won't be able to try it out for comfort or to see if it fits the horse or horses you'll be riding before you buy, and returning such large equipment can be a hassle.

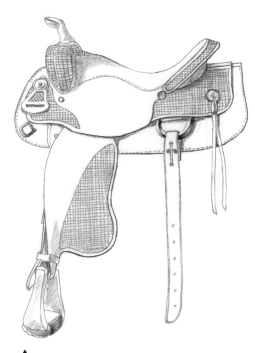

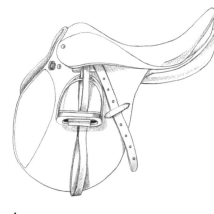

If you buy a saddle at your local tack shop, you'll probably be able to try it on your horse and even ride in it to make sure it fits both the horse and you.

Western Saddles

Among the Western saddles, there are models designed for trail riding, roping, barrel racing, reining, endurance riding, and more. Each is designed differently. Reining saddles, for instance, are supposed to be designed to help the rider maintain balance during the quick turns and sudden stops characteristic of the sport. The horn should be short so it doesn't get in the way of the rider's hand. A Western saddle made for trail riding features a well-padded seat for comfort, such as you'd want on a long trail ride.

English Saddles

As an English rider, you have just as many choices in saddles. If you take a class or two per week and maybe trail ride in between, an all-purpose saddle probably is your best bet. These saddles have a design that isn't too extreme in any way, which makes them suitable for a variety of activities.

If you take up jumping seriously, you'll want a jumping saddle. These have knee rolls that are further forward to accommodate the necessary position for jumping. Dressage riders ride with a longer stirrup length, so on dressage saddles, the stirrup leathers are further back than on other saddles, and the flaps on the saddle are longer to accommodate the rider's position. See the illustrations to understand the basic differences among some of the more common English saddles.

A Western trail saddle

An English all-purpose saddle, with stirrup leathers and irons

▶

Notice that the English jumping saddle (a) has a more forward shape compared with the dressage saddle (b), which has longer flaps. Both are designed to accommodate the rider's position for each sport.

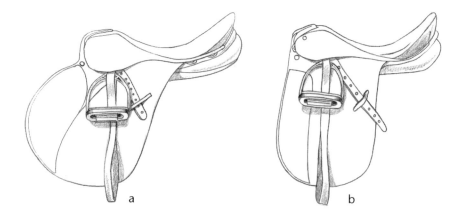

a   b

Checking Out a Saddle

Even if you can't afford a top-of-the-line saddle, look at a few in this category to get an idea of what a good saddle looks like. Then shop for the one that suits your budget. When you think you've found the saddle that's right for you:

- **Make sure the tree in the saddle is straight and that the stufing is even.** The tree is the internal frame of the saddle. If it's crooked, it will be uncomfortable for you and the horse. If the panels on the saddle are sewn on or stuffed unevenly, the saddle will sit off to one side, which can be unstable and make your horse sore. Make sure you deal with a knowledgeable saddle shop.

    To spot a crooked tree or uneven stuffing, hold the saddle upside down and perpendicular to the floor. Then look straight down the length of the saddle to see if it appears to be straight and evenly padded.

- **Check the billets or rigging.** The billets are those straps to which you attach the girth on an English saddle. In Western saddles, the place where the cinch attaches is called the rigging. Make sure the billets or rigging is attached securely to the saddle. (More on billets and rigging appears below.)

- **Try it out.** Many tack shops will let you take a saddle for a test run. Ride in the saddle. Don't just walk around. Trot, canter, and do whatever else you usually do to make sure it's comfortable.

- **Get an opinion.** Enlist the help of your instructor or someone else knowledgeable to determine whether the saddle fits your horse. Have this person also watch you ride in the saddle and get an opinion about whether the saddle is a good choice for you.

Leather or Synthetic?

Both English and Western saddles come in leather and synthetic materials.

Generally speaking, saddles made of leather from Germany, England, and France are considered of better quality by many riders than those from other places, such as Argentina and India.

Synthetic saddles, which are much less expensive than leather saddles, have improved a lot over the years and are lighter in weight than their leather counterparts. Some of the Western synthetics come in bright,

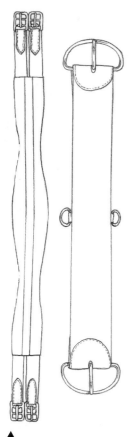

A typical English girth is on the left; a typical Western cinch is to the right.

attractive colors with matching saddle pads. Some people say that they don't hold up as well as a leather saddle, but I also know several riders who love their synthetic saddles for their light weight and comfort. See what appeals to you, and consider your budget.

Girths and Cinches

Girths and cinches are the equipment that holds the saddle on around the horse. English riders use girths (which attach to the billets) and Western riders use cinches (these attach to the rigging).

Synthetic cord girths usually cost about half what you'll spend for leather girths. Western cinches are comparable in price range. Considering that they hold on the saddle, girths and cinches are important pieces of equipment, so don't skimp too much.

If you're buying an English girth, do opt for one that's elasticized at one end — it makes it ever so much easier to get it on.

Where to Buy Equipment

As a novice, it's nice to shop at your local tack shops because the clerks will be there to show you around and provide some guidance. They are often riders themselves.

Once you know what you want, you may find some good bargains in one of the many horse equipment catalogs — but not always. Although the initial price of a product may be cheaper than what you pay in the tack store, catalogs usually charge for shipping and charge an additional fee for heavier items. It may or may not cost more than purchasing products at your local tack shop. Compare prices before you buy.

Stirrup Leathers and Irons

If you're buying an English saddle, you'll probably have to buy your stirrup leathers separately. Stirrup leathers get worn, so invest in a good pair that will hold up. Cheaper leathers tend to stretch so the holes become uneven, which is a nuisance.

Stirrup irons are another necessary purchase if you buy your own English saddle. Their cost varies widely.

Some safety experts advise "breakaway" irons for beginning English riders. These are designed to come apart under pressure to help ensure that your foot doesn't get caught when you take a spill. They'll cost more than an inexpensive pair of regular stirrups. Some have a rubber ring side that disengages; others are all stainless steel but have one side that comes loose. A third kind of safety stirrup is available that has no mechanical parts; it has one side that curves out, allowing more room for your foot to slide out.

There are rubber pads for stirrups to cushion your foot and give you some grip. Some stirrups come with the rubber pads; others do not. Stirrup pads cost as little as a few dollars. They do wear and you will need to replace them periodically.

Regular English stirrups may bother your feet. In this case, consider purchasing a pair of irons designed for endurance riders. They are wider under the ball of the foot than traditional stirrups and you might find them more comfortable, especially on long trail rides.

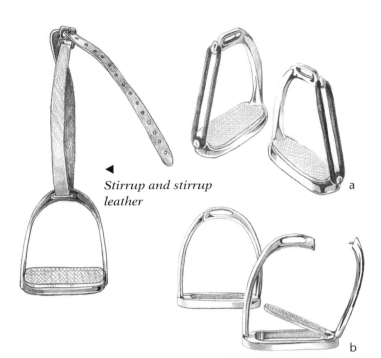

◄ *Stirrup and stirrup leather*

a

b

▲
The breakaway stirrup (a) has a rubber side designed to disengage under pressure; the breakaway stirrup (b) is all stainless steel and functions similarly.

Saddle Pads

A saddle pad should not interfere with the proper fit of the saddle, so seek some guidance before buying. Western pads usually are larger and thicker than their English counterparts. It's unlikely that a very thick Western saddle pad will work well with any English saddle, leather or synthetic, or that a thin English pad will work with a much heavier Western leather saddle.

English riders should consider the type of saddle. If you have a dressage saddle, you'll want a dressage saddle pad; other pads may not be large enough. Some pads are designed to be used with jumping saddles.

Western riders have the option of saddle "blankets" (these also are available for English saddles), which come in an array of lovely patterns.

There also are therapeutic saddle pads available for horses with special problems; you need not buy these unless advised to do so by your instructor or veterinarian.

An ordinary English saddle pad is relatively inexpensive. Those with fancy designs or stitching will cost more. Western saddle pads are similar in price, unless you opt for a really fancy model.

Used Tack

Many of us start out with used saddles and other tack. It's an excellent option if you have to watch what you spend. Many tack shops have a used section, and some tack shops specialize in used tack. Sometimes you can find a really well-made saddle that just needs some minor repairs. Ask around; you might even find people at your barn who want to upgrade their saddles or switch to another kind and will make a deal on their old equipment.

Wash saddle pads regularly; check the directions that come with the pad you buy. I've found that they hold up longer if you never put them in the dryer; hang them on a line or put them in the sun to dry.

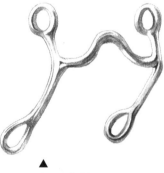

► *An English jumping saddle pad (a), an English dressage pad (b), and a Western saddle pad (c). Each is designed to be used with a specific type of saddle.*

a   b   c

Bits, Bridles, and Reins

The bit, bridle, and reins give you control over the horse while you're riding him. If you've been riding a horse with no problem and you want to buy your own bridle and bit, get the same type and the same size you've been using.

Bits

Bits, which rest on the bars (gums) of the horse's mouth and help you control the animal, come in almost limitless variety. The jointed snaffle bit is very common and is considered a mild bit. It's the type of bit that you're likely to find on a well-behaved horse appropriate for beginners. There are different types of cheek pieces that come with bits; a common type, and one of the most gentle, is the full-cheek snaffle.

Another type of bit is the leverage bit. This model is used with a "curb" strap or chain that fits under the horse's chin. It is considered a more severe bit than a jointed snaffle, but, of course, a lot depends on how you use a bit.

Generally, the thinner the bit, the more harsh it's, but it is possible to have a bit that is so fat that it's uncomfortable for the horse.

If you're buying anything other than exactly what has been used on the horse, it's imperative that you consult with your instructor or trainer first to make sure the bit you're getting is appropriate for the horse.

▲
A curb bit

Bridle

A bridle consists of a headstall, the bit, and reins; on English bridles, generally it includes the cavesson — the piece that goes around the nose. It can be confusing for the novice because sometimes the parts of bridles are sold à la carte.

The headstall goes over the horse's head behind the ears and includes the browband. You know what the bit and reins are. The cavesson goes over the horse's nose and isn't always necessary, unless you have a horse

that gapes his mouth open or you need it to attach to a
standing martingale. See the illustrations to understand
all the various parts and how they go together.

Most bridles are still leather, but they do come now in
a strong synthetic material with lovely bright colors. I'd
worry, however, that a synthetic bridle wouldn't break if
the horse got caught up on something, and for that
reason I use leather bridles; leather is more likely to
break if it's not too thick.

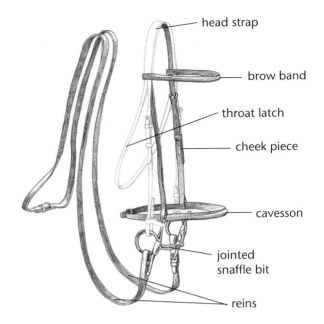

Reins

Check out the reins carefully. Some reins are leather,
and they come designed in a variety of ways. Others are
made of rubber. I've found some leather reins are hard to
hold on to, and I much prefer rubber reins. You might
not. Just try out different kinds of reins before you buy
them, because you are likely to have a preference.

*All these parts
equal a full bridle.*

Cavesson

This is the part of the bridle that goes around the horse's nose. English-
style riders, ask your instructor whether you really need a cavesson. If
you're going to show, you might. But if you have a well-behaved horse, and
you're strictly a pleasure rider, it's probably unnecessary. Western horses
seldom wear a cavesson; I ride English and never use a cavesson on either
of my horses. It's just one more piece of equipment to fool with and clean.

*A running martingale (a)
and standing martingale (b)*
▼

Nosebands and Martingales

This equipment is intended to give the rider more
control. A drop noseband keeps the horse from opening
his mouth and getting his tongue over the bit. A flash
noseband combines the cavesson and drop noseband; a
grakle noseband makes kind of a figure 8 over the horse's
nose. These are used for the same purpose as the drop
noseband — more control.

A standing or running martingale discourages a horse
from tossing or holding his head too high. The standing
martingale attaches to the cavesson noseband or a
cavesson with a flash (but generally not other types
of nosebands); the running martingale is attached to
the reins.

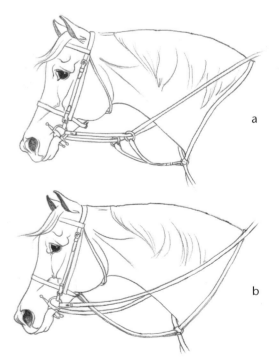

Halters

You use halters and leads when you're on the ground, to lead the horse. Halters come both in strong synthetic material and in leather. Either is fine for the times you'll simply be leading from point A to point B.

Never turn out a horse or leave him in a stall with a halter that won't break readily — like a nylon halter or a very thick leather halter. He could get his leg hung up in it scratching an ear or catch the halter on something. Horses need a safety halter (see box).

Halters can get very dirty when horses wear them for turnout — in the pasture — and roll in them, but many of them can be cleaned in the washer. Scrub first with a brush to get out ground-in dirt, then toss them in the machine with lots of old towels. They'll come out looking like new.

Halter Safety

Never leave a halter on a horse when he is in his stall. It's too easy for him to get the halter caught on something and injure himself. Many horsemen also believe that horses should never be turned out into a pasture with a halter on, but at some barns it's considered necessary to catch the horses.

If a horse is turned out with a halter on, he should have a safety or *break-away halter*. This is a halter with a leather crown piece that will break with force. There are a couple of types of breakaways. One has the leather crown piece affixed on one side with Chicago screws and a buckle on the other side. I don't like this kind; the screws always seem to work their way out, and even if you keep these little screws on hand, it seems you can never find them when you need them. The type of safety halter I recommend has buckles on both sides to attach the breakaway strap.

A regular leather halter is inadequate for turnout or stalling; if the leather is too thick, it might not break if the horse gets hung up.

It's also a good idea to use a safety halter any time a horse is tied to a post or is in cross ties.

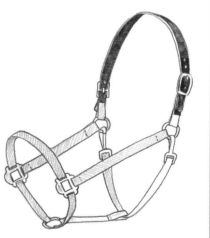

Leads

To lead the horse around, you use a rope with a snap on the end that attaches to the halter ring under the horse's chin. Some lead ropes have a chain between the lead and the snap; others don't. With a well-behaved horse, all you need is a rope lead, not a rope with a chain. (Don't ever tie a horse or graze a horse with a rope that has a chain; he could injure himself on the chain.) Do buy a lead rope that will give you a good grip. Some of them are flat instead of round, and can be hard to hang on to. I like a big thick round cotton rope; some of the round nylon ropes are nice, too, and probably will hold up better than cotton when they get wet.

Crops and Whips

A crop is a shorter version of a whip. You shouldn't use any kind of whip unless your instructor has advised you to, so it may not be a necessary item for you. Crops and whips are used to encourage a horse to move on or to obey other commands. Crops generally are used to tap the horse on the shoulder; whips usually are used to reinforce leg aids. Which you use depends on the horse and what you're trying to accomplish; your instructor will help guide you.

Crops come in handy on the trail for pushing brambles out of the way and for scaring off a bothersome dog. Whips aren't a good idea for trail riding: They get caught in bushes too easily.

When buying a crop or whip, find one that has a nice, thick handle that's easy to hold on to. Some are too slender and drop out of your hand easily.

Crops often have a loop handle, too, but don't put your hand through it — you want to be able to drop the crop quickly. In addition, if you get the handle caught on something, you could hurt your hand.

▲
A crop (a) and a whip (b)

Blankets

If a healthy horse is allowed to grow a winter coat, he probably doesn't need a blanket. (And if you blanket a horse too early in the season, he won't grow a good winter coat.)

Still, virtually all the horse owners I know want their horse blanketed overnight when the temperature dips low in winter. We worry that the horses will become uncomfortably cold overnight, either standing in the stall or in a pasture, because they aren't moving around as much as they do during the day when they romp and play. In the Mid-Atlantic region where I live, we generally blanket stalled horses overnight when temperatures dip below freezing.

Horses that have been clipped don't have a natural heavy hair coat to protect them and certainly do need blanketing in very cold weather. So do old or ill horses, who may be more vulnerable to chilling.

Blankets vary widely in design and purpose, so consider carefully what you need before buying, because they aren't cheap. Some blankets are meant for use in the stall only and are not intended for turnout; they aren't rugged enough to withstand the abuse they'll get on a horse running and playing in the field, and they often aren't waterproof. Others are designed for turnout and are rugged and waterproof. Waterproof blankets may not be "breathable" and hence may not be suitable for indoor use or in fluctuating temperatures.

The high-quality, more popular blankets for horses are expensive. But if you buy a cheaper blanket that doesn't hold up and have to replace it, you end up spending more in the long run. You may be able to get a break on the price of a blanket from tack shops if several of you get together and each buys one at the same time.

When buying blankets, watch the cut around the neck. Some are cut back farther on the shoulder and seem to pull on the chest; those cut higher on the neck look more comfortable.

Sheets and Coolers

Sheets and coolers are lighter than blankets. These products aren't a must, but they're still nice to have.

A rain sheet keeps rain off the horse when he's outside. It must be waterproof to do this, not just water-resistant, as some horse blankets are. Some sheets are lined for extra warmth. Sheets also keep a horse from getting very dirty when conditions are muddy, so grooming before a ride doesn't take as long.

There are a couple of kinds of coolers. One is called an anti-sweat sheet, and is made of cotton mesh or a cotton and polyester mesh; it's supposed to speed the horse's cooling down time without chilling. One popular type is the Irish mesh version. Other coolers are made of polar fleece and some of wool and acrylic; there are also varieties made of acrylic only. These can be nice to have when you're trying to get your horse cooled down after a workout in cold weather and you don't want him to get chilled, which may predispose him to illness.

Miscellaneous Equipment

Other equipment you want to have, especially if you buy a horse or are responsible for any horse's care and equipment, is listed below.

Fly Mask

This protects the horse's eyes from flies. Flies congregate around a horse's eyes because they feed on ocular discharges.

Several new styles of fly masks have emerged over the past few years. I've tried most of them, and for comfort on my horses and durability, none holds up as well as the first kind I ever bought before all these newcomers came out. It's the Farnam SuperMask and it's inexpensive. There's a separate ear cover you can purchase to go with the mask that costs just a little more.

It's easy to misplace a fly mask, and they get mixed up with others in a busy barn. I permanently identify mine by sewing on the horse's name in needlepoint.

Protective Leg Gear

Two of the most common types are bell boots and brushing boots. If the horse overreaches and hits the heels of his front feet with his back feet, for instance, bell boots might be a good investment. Brushing boots protect the inside of a horse's leg if he tends to knock one leg with the hoof of the other. You don't need horse boots unless your horse has a specific problem.

▲ *This Farnam SuperMask stays on well, is sturdy, and seems comfortable for most horses.*

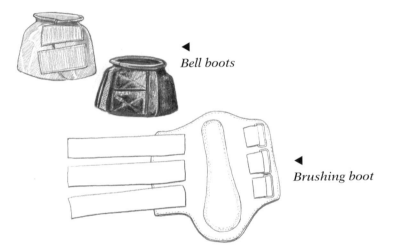

◀ *Bell boots*

◀ *Brushing boot*

Traveling Equipment

For transporting a horse, perhaps to a show or to a veterinary hospital, traveling equipment is essential. However, you may be able to borrow what you need, so ask around before investing, especially if you won't be transporting a horse too frequently. Another option is to share the cost with another rider who might need to use this equipment only occasionally.

A *head bumper* attaches to the halter and protects the horse's head in case he bumps his poll against the top of the trailer.

Shipping boots protect the most vulnerable part of the horse's legs during transport — the part below the knees, including the coronary band — in case he gets kicked by another horse in the trailer or accidentally kicks himself. Some people wrap the horse's legs with pillow wraps for this purpose. These fairly inexpensive wraps are held on by

▲ *When trailered, horses should wear head bumpers for protection.*

bandages (also reasonable) with hook and loop (Velcro) on the ends. If you're all thumbs, like I am, they are difficult to put on.

For about the same price, you can buy a set of fleece-lined shipping boots; these are all-in-one contraptions that you simply put on and affix with a hook-and-loop setup — no wrapping is needed.

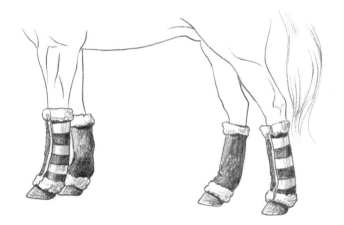

▶

For those of us who are all thumbs, these shipping boots are much easier to put on than are wraps and bandages!

A *tail wrap* (or a leg wrap used to wrap the tail and secured with duct tape) will protect the hair on the horse's upper tail. Sound unnecessary? I failed to wrap the top of my Quarter Horse's tail once during an hour-long jaunt to a veterinary clinic in Virginia, and when we got there the top of his beautiful tail was bald! He'd rubbed it against a bar in the trailer. Just a small outlay for the bandages and duct tape will avoid this. But don't wrap the tape too tight! It can impair circulation and damage the tail.

A *hay net* is something else you might need if you'll be taking the horse to a show or anywhere else where you'll want to be able to provide hay. You can buy one, but it's also something that's usually easy to borrow. A note of caution: Horses can get their legs caught up in a net — tie it high enough so that this can't happen, whether the net is empty or full.

A *bucket* is a must if you're taking your horse somewhere else to ride. It's healthier to bring your own bucket and fresh water than to let him drink from a communal-type watering trough. Shared water buckets can be the source of disease. A new bucket is an inexpensive purchase.

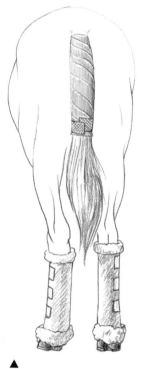

▲

Wrap a horse's tail if he's being trailered. Otherwise, he could rub off tail hair during transport.

Cleaning Tack

Tack is expensive, so you'll want to make it last by taking care of it. Clean it routinely. Take the time to check for worn places that could present a safety hazard to you. Cleaning tack once a week is often recommended, but I know few adult pleasure riders who are this vigilant. It really will depend on how often you ride, the conditions you're riding in, and how dirty the tack gets. When it starts to look dirty, clean it.

There are all sorts of ways to go about cleaning your tack; here's the simple way I do it.

For the saddle:
• Take off the stirrup leathers, remove the irons, and remove the pads from the irons.
• Use a soft, barely damp sponge or rag rubbed on a cake of saddle soap. Go over every inch of the saddle (including the bottom part, the billets — everything!).
• Now rub in some leather conditioner. I rub it in with my hand, let it dry, then polish with a clean soft cloth.
• Wash the stirrup irons and pads in warm, soapy water, then rinse and dry.
• If your tack needs it, go over the metal parts with some metal polish.

That's it!

The same saddle soap and conditioner can be used to clean the bridle. You'll also want to wash saddle pads routinely — I wash mine after every use and let them line dry or hang in the sun. Clean the girth regularly, too. Wipe and condition leather; girths made of nylon and other synthetics usually can be washed. I toss mine in the washer and then line dry.

The bit should be at least wiped after every use. I keep a box of moist towelettes in the car for this purpose. At other times, wash the bit in warm, soapy water. If there's caked-on dirt, it will come off easily with a nylon scrubber.

6 Basic Horse Care

Businesswoman Anne Warner took up riding regularly at age 36. She currently rides three times a week and enjoys many different types of riding activities.

"Riding is fun. It provides outdoor exercise. It's frequently challenging, and occasionally frustrating. It's also an excuse to get good and dirty! I enjoy the camaraderie with horses and the opportunity to socialize with other women."

To BE A RESPONSIBLE RIDER, you need to know how to care for a horse, but it's far from being a chore. It's one of the most enjoyable aspects of involvement with horses, because they happen to be not only beautiful, but also particularly interesting creatures.

A veterinarian pondering the species commented that horses are simple, complex creatures. Sound like a contradiction? Not really. Their needs are quite basic, but horses are at the same time complicated animals. You'll agree after you become more educated about them.

In this chapter, you'll learn about feeding, grooming, bathing, control of internal and external parasites, and other important, basic care that every horse is entitled to receive.

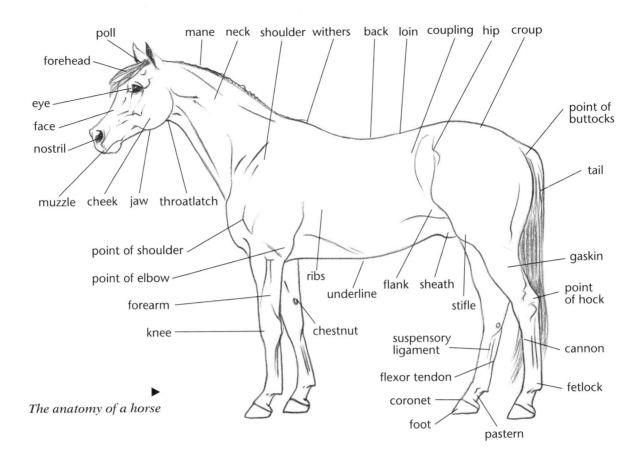

The anatomy of a horse

Feeding

Horses are herbivores; that is, they are animals that survive primarily by eating plants. In the wild, horses spend most of their time grazing continuously, eating small amounts at a time.

This is due to their anatomy. The horse may be a large animal, but he has a very small stomach. At most, it will hold about 4 gallons. The horse digests food most efficiently when the stomach is not full.

Horses that have ample access to good pasture may not need anything else to eat, because the pasture can provide the nutrients they need. Many horses, however, also need hay and some grain; if they are worked, they need more nutrients, and if they live in a stall much of the time, they don't have enough access to good pasture. Even horses that are on pasture all the time need other sources of nutrients at times when the grass isn't good, as might occur during summer droughts, during winter, or when there are many horses on little acreage and the pasture is overgrazed.

Proper feeding is essential, so before you take on the responsibility for feeding a horse, consult with an experienced horseman, a veterinarian, or feed dealer. This section will tell you about some of the basic principles you'll need to keep in mind.

Give Small Meals

Horses should never receive one large meal; they'll be too hungry and will gobble up their food, which can result in serious digestive problems. The better way to feed a horse is to provide several small meals a day — at least two and preferably three. Make changes in diet gradually, to avoid digestive upsets.

Just how much hay and grain a horse should receive is going to vary with the horse, how he is kept, and how hard he is worked. If a horse is accustomed to receiving 2 quarts of grain morning and evening, but then he has to be stalled due to an injury and can't get outside or be ridden, reduce the amount of grain during this time of inactivity.

Hay Is Good for Horses

Hay, like grass, provides roughage, which is important for horses and should account for the bulk of the food they eat to supplement grass in the pasture. It helps get their intestines moving, which reduces the risk of serious conditions such as colic (which you'll learn about in the next chapter).

Hay fed to horses must be fresh. Take great care never to feed a horse hay that is moldy. Some molds are toxic and can poison a horse. To prevent mold, store hay properly, and in a dry place.

Ask your instructor or an experienced horseman to show you good-quality hay, which has a sweet, fresh smell, as well as how to store hay. That way, you'll know good hay when you see it, and be able to spot poor-quality or moldy hay.

There are several types of hay. The most commonly fed to horses is grass hay, such as timothy hay. Another type of hay, known as a legume, is alfalfa hay, but it contains more nutrients and may be too rich for some horses, providing more protein than they require.

There's been some debate about when it's best to provide hay to horses before or after the meal, but most horsemen I know feed hay before they give grain. Hay fills the stomach partially, which discourages the gobbling of grain. It also is thought to help horses more completely digest the grain that follows.

▶

Hay, like grass, provides roughage, which is very important for horses and should account for the bulk of their diet.

Grain

Grains are also called concentrates. Unlike hay, they don't provide much fiber, but they are high in energy. Oats are a grain. Corn, another grain, contains more energy than oats.

Just as with hay, take care that grain is of good quality and free of mold.

Salt Blocks

Adequate salt intake is important to the health of horses. If they don't have enough salt, they can easily become exhausted or lose their appetite. Consequently, all horses should have access to a salt block or a mineral salt block (a salt block with added minerals that are good for horses).

Salt comes in large blocks about the size of a cinder block, which often are placed in the corner of a stall floor, and in small blocks, about the size of a brick, which are kept in special holders on the stall wall. Some horses won't lick a large block off the floor; the solution may be to build a shelf into the corner or buy a holder to get the block off the ground, or to switch to the smaller block that is intended to be mounted on a wall. You can provide salt in loose form if a horse just won't lick a salt block.

Commercial Rations

Many owners feed their horses commercial grain rations, which should provide all the nutrients a horse needs if they are high-quality rations. Some of these rations also contain hay. They come in many different forms. Loose grain that contains molasses, which makes it more palatable to the horse, is called sweet feed. There are also feeds that are compressed into cubes; others are processed into pellets.

Some veterinarians and horsemen believe that pelleted feeds are not the best choice for healthy, mature horses because they are processed, which doesn't satisfy the horse's need to chew roughage; consequently, they say, pellets are associated with undesirable behavior such as fence chewing and cribbing. The horse's digestive system also is designed to process roughage.

Pellets, however, are easy to store and may be less likely to spoil in summer. They may also be necessary for some horses; old equines with missing teeth, for example, usually find it easier to chew processed food.

▲
Pelleted feed is on the left. On the right is sweet feed.

Supplements

A lot of owners give their horses an ounce or two of vegetable oil in their grain, which promotes a glossy hair coat. It's an inexpensive way to get a shine.

There are also all sorts of supplements on the market — typically, powdered products that you add to grain. A horse who is healthy and receiving a good diet doesn't need a supplement. Most commercial feeds are nutritionally balanced. When you add a little of this and that, it may throw things out of whack.

Water Is Crucial

Water promotes efficient food utilization and is vital to the horse's health. If horses don't get enough water, they can develop intestinal impaction. Horses should have access to water at all times. On average, horses drink about 10 gallons of water a day; when they are hot or have worked hard, they may drink as much as 20 gallons daily.

Grooming

Grooming horses helps keep their coats healthy. It stimulates the skin and removes excess dirt and scurf, which is scaly, dry skin. Grooming also removes dirt that could rub and irritate the horse's skin in the saddle and girth area.

There are other reasons for grooming. It's an opportunity to inspect the coat for parasite eggs, cuts, lumps, bumps, and other skin problems that might not be readily apparent otherwise.

Cleaning out the hooves is an important part of grooming. It minimizes the likelihood of disease, and it's the only way to be certain that there are no stones or sticks lodged in the foot.

Grooming also provides a chance for horse and rider simply to be together and get to know each other better. It should be a pleasant experience for both.

How Often to Groom

Ideally, horses should be groomed daily. In reality, most are thoroughly groomed before they are ridden, and get "touch-ups" in between. Touch-ups include some brushing and always a hoof-cleaning. If your horse's coat is healthy and he hasn't gotten too dirty, a thorough grooming a few times a week with touch-up brushing in between probably is adequate. However, the hooves still should be cleaned out daily or as often as possible, especially if your horse is stalled, because he's likely to step in manure and his "wet" or urine spot, which is bad for the feet.

Grooming Tools

All the tools you could use for grooming would make up a very long list, so I'll present only those I've found most useful.

The following are the bare essentials for ordinary, everyday grooming before riding (not bathing). The prices will vary for each grooming tool depending on the quality of the product you buy.

Essentials

These tools will help you keep your horse happy and healthy:

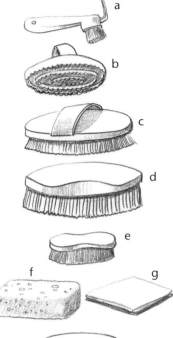

- Hoof pick (a), to clean out the feet
- Rubber curry (b), to loosen dirt on the coat above the knees
- Body brush (c) (medium stiff), to brush off the dirt
- A dandy or mud brush (d) (stiff), for removing mud and for grooming below the knee, where you don't want to use a curry
- Small face brush (e), gentle enough to brush the delicate area below the knee
- Medium-size sponge (f), for wiping around eyes and the nose, or a washcloth or dishcloth (g)
- Hairbrush (h) with rounded ends, for mane and tail

Note: Unless you have very large hands, buy brushes that are small; the very large kind have a tendency to fly out of your hand. The small brushes are sometimes called pocket-size.

Select a hoof pick carefully, because some of them are useless. A metal pick with a brush is nice and works better than a thick plastic pick.

Nonessential but Nice

The following grooming tools are nice to have and will enable you to do an even better job of grooming:

- Finishing brush (soft), for picking up any fine dust left on the coat after grooming
- Shedding blade, for removing shedding hair and heavy, caked-on mud above the knees
- Conditioner (e.g., Show Sheen), for tangled manes and tails

---

Identify Your Equipment

In a barn, where there generally are lots of people with similar equipment, it's easy to lose your grooming tools or for someone to inadvertently pick up yours and misplace them, so put your name on everything as soon as you purchase it!

Try sticking address labels on all your grooming equipment, then cover each label with clear tape so the print doesn't wear off. You can use the same method to identify things like crops and your helmet.

How to Groom

You'll probably develop your own routine for grooming, but here's one to get you started:

1. Using the rubber curry in a circular motion to loosen dirt and scurf, start at the top of the horse's neck and work backwards down one side of the horse on areas above the knees. (Then repeat down the other side.) Be very gentle over bony areas.

   There are a couple of kinds of rubber curries available. The most typical is oval and has two rows of "teeth" around. Another has "fingers" that also massage the horse as you curry. Different horses prefer different curries. One of mine will not tolerate the "massage" version; the other prefers it to the traditional rubber curry.

2. Follow with a medium-stiff brush to remove the loosened dirt and scurf. Use short, flicking motions in the same direction that the hair coat grows. (Periodically rub the rubber curry and brush against each other to clean off the dirt.)

3. Use the stiff mud or dandy brush from the knees down.

4. On the face, use only a soft brush designed for this purpose.

   Use your fingers to rub off dirt close to the eyes, or wear pimple gloves — also called barn gloves — that have little dots on the palm. You're less likely to poke the horse in the eye than you are using the face brush.

5. If the horse will allow, use the soft brush for cleaning the outside back of the ears.

6. Use a dampened sponge or soft washcloth to remove dirt on the face, around the eyes, and for cleaning out nostrils.

Warning! Don't use anything small enough to get lodged in the nose. I once used a wad of cotton; it got caught in my horse's nostril, which caused a real panic in both of us until I got it out.

Grooming Tips

- Groom gently! Many horses do not like to be groomed vigorously and prefer the gentle touch. If a horse appears to be fidgeting or misbehaving while you're grooming, you might be grooming too vigorously.
- For heavily caked mud, use a shedding blade first to remove it before using the rubber curry and brush. Be very gentle over bony areas or avoid them altogether with this tool.
- Be especially careful to groom well around the saddle and girth areas. After grooming, feel with your bare hand to make sure you didn't miss any caked-on dirt that could lead to irritation.
- If your barn has a vacuum for cleaning horses and the horse you are grooming is tolerant of it, you won't have to do as much brushing.

Cleaning Out the Hooves

Clean out each foot with a hoof pick, and work from the heel toward the toe as much as possible. If you work from the toe toward the heel and the pick slips, you can really stab yourself. Pay special attention to the crevices around the frog, the triangle-shaped part of the bottom of the horse's hoof.

Grooming the Mane and Tail

When the mane is really dirty, make it your first grooming chore. Otherwise, you'll brush dirt from the mane all over the horse you've just cleaned. Here's my favorite method for grooming the mane and tail:

1. About once a week, spray the mane and tail hair with a conditioner (e.g., Show Sheen). The effects of these products seem to last for at least a week, so there's usually no need to apply one more often. (If the horse objects to having his mane sprayed, spray the product on your hand and then apply. On the tail hair, apply the product below the actual tail of the horse, where the hair tends to tangle.)
2. Let the product dry completely.
3. Working from the bottom up, comb out mane, then tail, with a regular hairbrush for people. Choose one with widely spaced bristles and rounded ends. This causes less hair breakage than would a comb.
4. If the mane or forelock becomes especially dirty in winter when you can't bathe the horse, clean a small section at a time with a dampened warm washcloth; dry each area with a clean, dry towel.

Grooming After Your Ride

After you remove your horse's tack, you don't need to completely groom again, but it's a good idea to use the rubber curry and brush to remove marks left on the coat under the saddle. Be certain to clean and check out the hooves again.

If the horse has been sweating and his coat is wet in the saddle area, cool him down and let the hair coat dry before this after-ride grooming session. On a very hot day when the horse has been sweating heavily, start by sponging off the saddle area with water. Follow with a sweat scraper to remove excess water, let the horse dry, then curry as necessary and brush.

Removing Burrs

If your horse's mane and tail are tangled with burrs, spray or rub in a conditioner and let it dry completely. These products often make it possible to brush burrs right out with minimal hair breakage or to pick out burrs easily with your hands. To extract burrs, pull small strands of hair out of the burr, instead of trying to pull burrs out of the hair.

Extra Grooming

Even if you're riding just for pleasure and not for show, you may want to do some extra grooming from time to time to give your horse a neater appearance.

1. Use a finishing or very soft brush on the coat after the rubber curry and medium-stiff brush to remove fine dust and leave a shinier coat.
2. Clip off whiskers on the muzzle. Try to determine whether your horse is tolerant of scissors and electric clippers. If you can't find out, ask for help and proceed cautiously; some horses need to be conditioned gradually to the use of clippers.
3. Cut out a bridle path or neaten up an existing bridle path. A bridle path is a section of mane cut out where the bridle or halter goes over the top of the head. It shouldn't be more than about 2 inches wide. To do this, I use scissors first, then the electric clippers.
4. Clip around the edge of the ears. Avoid clipping hair that's within the ears; it helps keep out bugs.
5. Clip long hair from behind the fetlocks.

    Caution: This could dangerous for novices. Don't attempt this on your own the first time. Ask an experienced person to show you how and be sure your horse will cooperate.
6. Pull the mane. (Have someone show you how to do this.) It's best done after exercise, when the horse's pores are more likely to be open and the hair comes out more easily. Be aware that for some breeds, such as the Morgan, a full mane may be required for shows. An alternative to pulling the mane is braiding it.

▲
Clipping whiskers around the muzzle, trimming ears and behind the fetlock are all ways to neaten up a horse's appearance, but make sure your horse is tolerant of clippers. Some aren't.

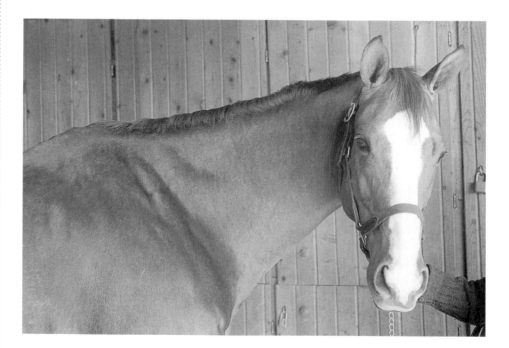

▶
This horse has a neatly pulled mane.

Bathing a Horse

Giving a full bath periodically helps keep a horse clean, makes grooming easier, and keeps saddle pads cleaner. You don't want to overbathe, however, which can remove natural oils that are good for the horse's skin.

How Often to Bathe

At my barn, we bathe horses in the spring once the weather heats up, give maybe one or two more baths during the peak summer months if a horse becomes really dirty, and give one more bath in early fall before the weather gets cold. Three or four baths a year should be adequate for most horses.

Bathing Weather

Some horse authorities say it's safe to bathe a horse as long as it's over 50 degrees outside; others say 60 degrees. I wait until it's at least 75 degrees, because I have to bathe my horses outside and have no hot water source. The horses must be rinsed with cold hose water, so I wait for a really warm, sunny day with no wind to reduce the risk of chilling.

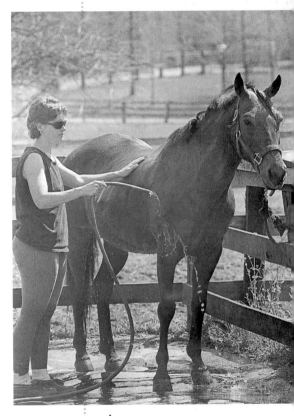

▲
Like grooming, bathing a horse should be a pleasant experience for both you and the animal.

Water Temperature

Maybe you'll be lucky enough to have a barn with an indoor wash stall with warm water and a place where the horse can dry out without exposure to chilly winds. If this is the case, use water that feels comfortably warm when applied to your wrist.

If you don't have access to hot water, let several buckets of water warm in the sun, or haul a few gallons of hot water and use them to warm partially filled buckets of cold water; use this warmed water for the initial dousing of the horse's body.

Shampoo Selection

The brand of shampoo you select doesn't much matter, in my experience. Unless you have a horse with a special condition that requires a medicated shampoo, one shampoo is as good as another.

There are a couple of situations in which you might want to use something different. One is the initial spring bath. Many owners like to use a shampoo that contains iodine, or they simply add some iodine to the soapy water for that first bath of the year to really clean the coat after a long winter. Ask your instructor or another expert to show you how much iodine to add, since too much may irritate the skin. The iodine also helps reduce the risk of fungal skin conditions, which are not uncommon during damp spring weather.

If your horse is white, or has white socks, stockings, or a blaze, the special purple shampoos designed for whitening really do help brighten these areas.

Bathing Tools and Procedure

Tools for bathing include:

- A 5-gallon bucket, to hold soapy water
- Bottle of shampoo
- Extra medium-size sponge, for cleaning around the dock
- Sweat scraper, for removing excess water after bathing

If you want to get fancy, you can also invest in:

- Grooming scissors, for various trimming jobs
- Electric clippers, for trimming the muzzle and bridle path — the place where the bridle or halter rests behind the horse's ears

Following is my method for bathing a horse.

1. Properly restrain the horse according to the rules at your barn, which might be in cross ties or to a post in a wash stall. Wherever it is, you should be next to a hose, and the footing should be something the horse won't slip on.
2. Groom the horse to loosen dirt.
3. Wet the horse's legs first with the hose to get him used to the feeling of the water.
4. Use the warm water, from either the hose or your warmed buckets, to soak him from the neck and chest area back, avoiding the head.
5. Add shampoo to a bucket, then add water. Dip in a large sponge, then start shampooing the horse. Don't apply shampoo directly to the horse from the bottle; it's too hard to rinse out.
6. Shampoo systematically. For instance, working on the left, shampoo the chest, the throat area, the neck, shoulder, front left

leg, and so on until you've completely washed one side, including underneath the horse. In mares, don't neglect the folds of the udders. Rinse thoroughly. Repeat for the other side.

7. With your fingers, shampoo the base of the mane at the crest of the neck; using only the sponge here won't get it clean.

8. Gently wash the area around the anus and the back of the legs. When rinsing here, take care not to squirt water directly at this sensitive area; rinse by letting water run down the back of the horse.

9. Wash the dock and the rest of the tail with your soapy sponge, then gently scrub with your fingers. Wash the tail hair below the tail by dunking it in your bucket of soapy water. Rinse very well.

10. Wash the face. I prefer a washcloth here, using plain water above and around the eyes. If the horse has a dirty blaze, I use a very slightly soaped washcloth well below the eyes and down, and rinse the area with a clean, wet washcloth.

11. Remove excess water on the body with a sweat scraper (avoid bony parts and the face with this tool).

12. Let the horse dry in the sun if there's no wind; under windy conditions, put a cooler on him to prevent chilling.

Using conditioner on the horse's body after bathing is not a necessity, but many owners feel it makes a horse's coat nicer. Conditioner applied to the mane and tail will make combing out much easier. Some conditioners require rinsing, so be sure to read the directions.

▲
A sweat scraper helps remove sweat or excess water after bathing, and the horse will dry faster, too. To facilitate soap removal, shampoo, then scrape, then rinse.

Cleaning a Sheath

The pocket of skin that houses the male horse's penis is known as the sheath. It gets dirty with a black, greasy, sebaceous material called smegma.

If smegma accumulates too much, it can cause irritation of the sheath. Sometimes it accumulates at the end of the penis, forming a little ball known as a bean, which can interfere with urination. The same material will build up on the penis, and you can see it when the horse drops the penis out of the sheath to urinate.

If a male horse is rubbing his tail for no apparent reason, he may have an irritated, dirty sheath that needs cleaning. Male horses should have their sheaths cleaned as needed; in many horses, that translates into about twice yearly, but some may need cleaning more often.

Before you try to clean a sheath for the first time, be sure the horse tolerates the procedure. If you're not certain, ask someone who is experienced to help you out and supervise the first time around. Some horses need one hind leg held up to prevent them from kicking.

To clean the sheath, you can use one of the products designed for this purpose; ask your veterinarian for her recommendation. Just don't use anything harsh, such as soaps that contain iodine, which could irritate the sheath.

Wear a tight-fitting latex or rubber surgical glove. Very gently hose water into the sheath. Put the soap or special cleanser onto the palm of your hand, stick your hand up into the sheath, and start gently soaping and removing the smegma.

Smegma can be really tough to get out; when this is the case, try this tip from *How to Be Your Own Veterinarian (sometimes),* by Dr. Ruth B. James (see recommended reading): Rub mineral oil into the sheath thoroughly and let it set overnight. Wash the sheath the next day as described above.

The horse's penis also should be washed. If you're lucky, you'll be able to gently pull it down for cleaning. Getting the horse to drop can be difficult, however, and you might want to ask for help from someone experienced.

Hoof Care

The hooves are part of the horse's feet. They cover sensitive internal structures and act as shock absorbers. Hooves grow continuously, just as our fingernails do. Check out the illustrations of the hoof on pages 99 and 100 to understand its complexity.

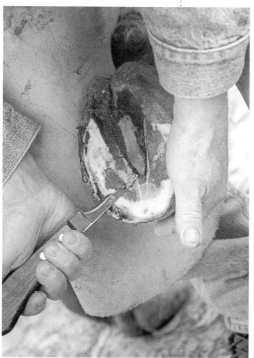

▲
Regular hoof trimming from a farrier is an important part of routine horse care.

The most cogent explanation of the importance of hoof care I've seen is in the *Horse Owner's Veterinary Handbook,* by James M. Griffin, M.D., and Tom Gore, DVM (see recommended reading): ". . . the hoof is a dynamic organ. With improper care, the foot breaks down and the horse is useless. A good program of regular inspection, cleaning, trimming and shoeing will prevent most hoof problems." (page 254)

In other words, the old adage "No hoof, no horse" really is true. If the horse's feet break down and he goes lame, you can't ride him. That's why it's important to take care of his hooves.

You've already learned that keeping the horse's feet clean by picking them out regularly can help prevent injuries and the development of disease. A good diet also is necessary to keep hooves healthy. So is having the horse's hooves trimmed and, for most horses, having them shod, too.

To understand why domesticated horses require hoof care, let's compare them to horses in the wild. In the wild, horses run over vast and varied terrain. It helps keep their feet clean, and it naturally wears down the hooves and toughens them.

Horses that are stalled some of the time and even horses kept outdoors on pasture can't keep their feet as clean, and they don't wear down their feet in the same way that their wild counterparts do. Their hooves need to be cleaned regularly. They must be routinely trimmed to keep the length in check and to keep them in balance. Domesticated horses also can't toughen their feet, which we stress by riding and working them. Consequently, they often need shoes to protect their feet.

In cooler weather, horses generally should be trimmed and reshod about every 6 to 8 weeks. In summertime, the hooves grow faster and may need attention as often as every 4 weeks.

The person who trims and shoes horses is called a farrier. See the box for more information about this important person.

Farrier

The professional who trims and shoes horses is called a farrier, but well-trained, experienced farriers do a lot more. They have vast knowledge about the anatomy of the horse, especially the feet and legs, and are expert in identifying lameness and in treating ailments of the equine foot.

In some areas, good farriers are in short supply, so they're very busy. Consequently, many owners set up a regular schedule for having their horses trimmed and shod instead of waiting until a horse needs attention. When the farrier is expected, the horse should be ready and waiting, not out in the pasture running around. Time is money, and if the farrier has to hang around idle while the owner goes to fetch the horse, he might find better ways to spend his time.

The best way to find a good farrier is to ask experienced horse owners, instructors, or barn owners. It's also a good idea to use a farrier with certification from a professional farrier organization. One of the oldest, largest, and the one with the toughest certification standards is the American Farriers Association. The highest level of certification is the certified journeyman farrier, designated after the farrier's name by CJF.

▲

To find a good farrier, ask experienced horse owners, instructors, or barn owners for their recommendations.

Hoof Products

There are lots of products on the market that are supposed to improve the condition of the hooves. Some are food supplements; others are hoof polishes and oils. However, unless your horse has a specific problem and one of these products is recommended by your veterinarian or farrier, they just aren't necessary, so save your money.

Teeth

A horse's adult or permanent teeth are all in place by age 5. The adult male horse can have up to forty-four teeth; a mare, from thirty-six to forty. Interestingly, a horse's teeth continue to growth throughout most of the animal's life.

The teeth in the front are called the *incisors.* Next, there's a space called the bars; that's where the bit rests in the horse's mouth. Then come the *premolars,* and then the *molars.*

Male horses also grow four *canine teeth* in the interdental space — one on each side of the top of the mouth, and one on each side of the lower mouth. Many horses also grow something called *wolf teeth* as their first premolars. Wolf teeth can cause discomfort when a bit is in place, and often are removed.

To eat, a horse bites off his food, such as grass, with the incisors, then grinds it with his premolars and molars before swallowing. During the grinding phase, he moves his lower jaw up and down and from side to side against the upper jaw. That side-to-side motion can result in the development of sharp edges on both the premolars and the molars. Generally, these edges are on the outside, or next to the cheek, of the upper teeth, and on the lower teeth they are on the tongue-side of the teeth.

The edges can cause discomfort and may interfere with the ability of the horse to chew, which you'll notice if he starts dropping feed out of his mouth while eating. They can cause discomfort when horses have the bit in their mouth, leading to head-tossing while you're riding. The male horse's canine teeth can also become quite sharp.

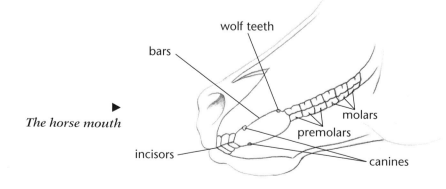

▶
The horse mouth

Signs of Tooth Problems

There are several signs that a horse has developed sharp edges and needs his teeth checked. They include:

- Dropping feed from the mouth while eating
- Poor body condition
- Chunks of undigested food in the stool
- Excessive salivation
- Disobedience under saddle, such as failure to stop or turn

To resolve these problems, have the horse's teeth checked, and filed if necessary. The process of filing teeth is called floating. It's usually done with a tool called a rasp — a big long file — although some other instruments are now available.

Your veterinarian can check the horse's teeth during routine visits to administer vaccines. There are equine dentists who specialize in care of the horse's teeth; some are quite accomplished, but others may not have much skill at all. If you want to use an equine dentist, first get a recommendation from a veterinarian you trust to help ensure that your horse receives quality care.

Aging Horses

It's long been thought that you can determine the age of an adult horse by looking at his teeth. There are two ways: One is to look for something called Galvayne's Groove, which is a groove that starts at the gum line on the corner incisor. When it shows up, a horse is thought to be about 10 years old. As the horse ages, the groove moves down the tooth. By the time it's all the way down, a horse is thought to be about 20 years old.

Another way to judge a horse's age is to check out the lower incisors. Horses have dental cups — little dents — on their upper and lower front teeth. With age and wear, these cups disappear, but there's a little dark dot called a dental star. The incisors also change their shape, becoming more triangular.

The accuracy of aging a horse by his teeth has come into question, however. In a British study by J. O. Richardson et al. published in 1995, researchers asked four experienced veterinarians to age more than 430 Thoroughbreds based on photos of their teeth. The researchers knew the true age of the horses, but the veterinarians did not. "The results show that the aging of horses from their [teeth] is an imprecise science ... [that] can provide no more than an 'informed guess,'" the researchers concluded. Obviously, the veterinarians weren't able to age the horses very accurately.

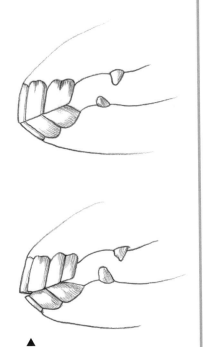

▲

The horse on the top is about 10 years old, judging by Galvayne's Groove. The horse on the bottom is about 20.

Internal Parasite Control

Internal parasites are a major threat to horses. They live out their life cycle within the horse and in the process cause serious anemia and weight loss, can damage the circulatory system and the gut, and, consequently, can be an important cause of colic.

Here's how horses generally get them: A horse with worms passes worm eggs in the stool. The manure, in turn, contaminates grass in the pasture or hay placed on the stall bedding, and the horse ingests the eggs. It's a vicious cycle, so you can never completely rid a horse of worms. Your goal is to keep the worm population in a horse at a level where it can't do serious damage.

The good news is that controlling internal parasites is possible by simply administering a tube of worming paste routinely. (See page 86 for a sample worming schedule.)

Types of Internal Parasites

There are all sorts of internal parasites that affect horses. Bloodworms, also known as strongyles, come in two basic varieties: large and small. Large strongyles are considered more damaging than small strongyles. They live in the intestines of the horse, including the bowel, and in the process of their life cycle they actually enter arteries.

Other types of worms that affect horses include roundworms (ascarids), threadworms (strongyloides), and pinworms *(Oxyurisequi)*, but these tend to be a problem more in young horses.

Tapeworms are another internal parasite affecting horses. They, too, are thought by some to be a problem of young horses, but they affect adult horses, too. When they do affect adults, the results can be very serious, such as intestinal perforations. So don't ignore tapeworms.

Stomach bots is an internal parasitic infection that is caused by the larvae of a bot fly. The fly lays eggs on the horse's coat. You can see the eggs: They are tiny yellow dots. These eggs hatch into larvae, which are licked by the horse, thus transporting them into the mouth. The horse then swallows them. The larvae attach themselves to the lining of the stomach, where they can cause ulcers or life-threatening inflammation of the lining.

Signs of Worms

Here are signs that a horse is infected with too many parasites:

- Dull hair coat
- Loss of condition
- Loss of appetite
- Weight loss
- Tail rubbing
- Diarrhea
- Colic

Worming Products

The products used to keep worms and bots to a minimum are called anthelmintics, wormers, or dewormers. Most owners use a paste, which is easily squirted into the horse's mouth.

There are several kinds, but I'm going to stick to two of the most widely used — pyrantel pamoate and ivermectin — to make it easy to understand worming and worming schedules. Consider the following:

1. Some wormers kill some types of internal parasites but not others. For example, pyrantel pamoate (Strongid) is effective against strongyles, and if administered in the higher-than-usual dose, it is also effective against tapeworms. It is *not* effective against bots, however. Ivermectin (Zimecterin, Eqvalan, Equimectrin) is highly effective against bots and strongyles, but it is not considered effective against tapeworms. For this reason, you can't use either product exclusively. If you do, you won't control all the internal parasites.
2. The development of resistance to wormers is a concern. One way to prevent resistance is to rotate the wormers you use.
3. Wormers must be fresh and stored properly to be effective.

Another type of worming product you should know about is pyrantel tartrate (Strongid C), formulated to be given daily to horses in their feed. It's supposed to reduce the incidence of colic. You also still need to worm horses for bots periodically with a product such as ivermectin.

At this writing, a new worming product called moxidectin (Quest) has just come on the market. It claims to protect against strongyle eggs longer than ivermectin. Check with a veterinarian first, however, before changing from a tried-and-true worming routine.

Horses also can be wormed by the veterinarian, who administers a wormer via a tube passed into the stomach, but most horse owners today use pastes.

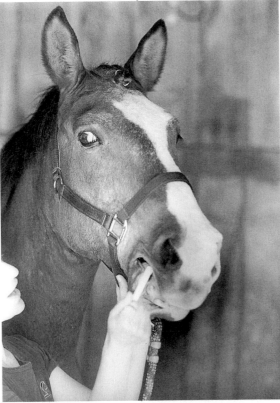

▶

Worming a horse is easy. It simply requires squirting a tube of paste into his mouth. After administering the paste, hold the horse's head up a few minutes to help ensure that he swallows it. Before worming, make sure there's no food in the horse's mouth. He might wad it up with the paste and spit it all out.

Worming Schedule

A commonly recommended routine is to administer a wormer at least every 8 weeks, and to rotate the products you use. Ideally, all horses on a farm should be wormed at the same time; this reduces reinfection.

It's important that you get a recommendation for worming from the veterinarian serving your barn or your horse. The schedule advised may vary depending on your geographic area and also on the horse's risk of exposure. For example, if there are many horses living on few acres of pasture, or if all horses on the farm aren't wormed at the same time, worming every 6 instead of 8 weeks may be recommended.

The double dose of pyrantel pamoate is advised by some veterinarians because at this dose, it's supposed to be effective against tapeworms. Don't give a double dose of anything, however, unless specifically advised to by your own veterinarian; studies have shown that pyrantel pamoate paste at this dose is safe, but a double dose of some other wormers may not be. This schedule also incorporates ivermectin enough to ensure that you'll be tackling the problem of bots.

SAMPLE WORMING SCHEDULE

To help you understand a worming schedule, the 8-week worming program recommended by a veterinary clinic in my area is listed below.

January 1	Ivermectin
March 1	Ivermectin
May 1	Double dose of pyrantel pamoate paste
July 1	Ivermectin
August 1	Ivermectin
October 1	Double dose of pyrantel pamoate paste
December 1	Ivermectin

(and so on)

Controlling Internal Parasites

Here's how to help control internal parasites:

- Worm horses regularly.
- Practice good manure management. This includes cleaning stalls daily and keeping pastures free of manure pileups.
- Remove bot eggs when you see them. I prefer a bot block, which is like a pumice stone that's rubbed on the hair coat where the eggs are found, to a bot knife.
- Have a stool sample examined periodically.

When the veterinarian comes to administer vaccines, it's a good idea to ask that the horse's stool be checked. (It's not expensive.) If the worming program is working, there should be a minimal amount of worm eggs found in the sample. A higher count may require a change in the worming program.

External Parasite Control

In regions where the weather gets hot, you're going to be battling flies and gnats. Investing in pest-control products is a must to keep horses comfortable. Pests can cause significant skin irritation, and when plentiful they will drive a horse nuts. Horses also can injure their legs and feet stomping to get flies off. As mentioned previously, bot flies also cause internal parasitic infection.

Let's hope you are riding at a barn with a pest-control system in place. This includes daily removal of manure from stalls and management of manure on the property. Manure piles should be removed from the area near the barn; manure in fields can be spread, enabling the sun to kill fly eggs.

Automatic Systems

For control within stalls, there are automatic systems that periodically emit a mist of a pest-control product that kills flies but is harmless to horses. Some barns have a barnwide system; if not, you can buy one of these devices for an individual stall. You'll need the device, batteries, and a spray canister that contains the pest-control product. The spray canister should last about a month, and the whole setup is inexpensive.

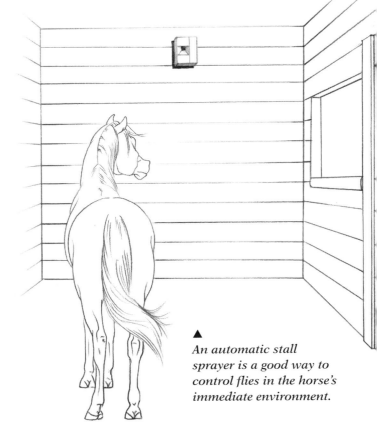

▲
An automatic stall sprayer is a good way to control flies in the horse's immediate environment.

Sprays for Horses

Horses also will most likely need to be sprayed (or wiped, depending on the product) with fly and gnat repellent before they go out to the pasture, where flies are more plentiful. The grass, too, seems to be where gnats like to congregate, waiting to attack your horse's ears and belly.

There are all sorts of sprays out there. The insecticides that also contain citronella, a natural bug repellent, seem to be popular. In the past few years, a number of "all-natural" herbal products have emerged. The more traditional products with citronella and the herbal products have a nice scent; unscented fly sprays have a horrid insecticide smell that's offensive to some people.

Don't bother with the least expensive varieties; I've found that they're just not effective. None of these products seem to last very long. Still, fly repellents often are necessary, and they will give your horse temporary relief.

The cost will add up, though: You may have to buy several bottles for one summer season. (I average 3 or 4 quarts per horse per year.) It's more economical to buy a concentrate, which you mix with water. These tend not to be scented pleasantly, however, as many of the ready-to-spray products are.

When spraying your horse with fly repellent, do it systematically. Start on one side at the top of the horse's neck and work your way down one side. There are wipes you can apply to the face (away from the eyes), or you can spray some repellent on a cloth and wipe it on.

After you're done, stand there and watch for about 1 minute; if you missed a place, you can tell because flies will land there. Spray where you missed.

Tape and Traps

Other traditional methods of controlling flies include fly-catcher tape and disposable traps — bags or plastic containers that are filled with water and a sex pheromone that attracts flies. Change these traps as soon as they are filled; if you don't, the stench of dead flies will overwhelm you. Tape and traps will reduce, but won't eliminate, the fly population within barns.

Protective Gear

Fly masks are an excellent way to keep flies off a horse's face while he's in the pasture. You can also buy ear covers (see below).

Some horses are so bothered by flies that they need even more protection, such as a scrim sheet — a lightweight sheet that keeps flies off a horse while he's in the pasture or his stall. There are even leg wraps designed to keep flies off the lower legs of horses; these are a good idea for an animal that is so bothered by flies that he stomps continually, which puts him at risk for traumatizing his feet and legs.

Really effective fly control is going to require a combination of good manure management, spraying horses, protecting them with fly masks or more if necessary, and using the automatic stall sprayers and fly traps.

Under saddle, a horse that hasn't been sprayed with repellent on a day that the flies and gnats are bad will be so distracted swatting, twitching, and shaking his head that you're likely to have a miserable ride. So when the flies are out, spray your horse thoroughly with repellent before you ride.

You don't want to spray his face; instead, invest in one of those cotton and crocheted ear and forehead covers. These are especially good for trail riding, where deerflies may be plentiful and tend to go for the ears; tassles on the edge of the mask help keep flies off the eyes. Spray the ear part of the cover well with fly repellent before putting it on.

Wipe repellent on parts of the face in areas that aren't too close to the eyes.

▶

A crocheted ear and forehead cover is a great way to help keep flies off your horse's ears and eyes during a ride.

Alternative Systems

Manure management should always be part of a good pest-control system, but some alternatives have emerged that may reduce or eliminate the need for spraying horses with repellents.

In-Feed Product

There are in-feed products — products you add to the horse's grain — that help control flies. They contain an ingredient that passes through the digestive system, without absorption, and prevents the development of stable and house flies in manure. They are supposed to be safe for horses as well as for wildlife or for dogs and cats that might come in contact with the manure of horses fed the product.

People I know who have used these products say they seem to reduce the fly population but do not completely eliminate the need for spraying with repellent.

These products are sold in tack shops and catalogs.

Biological Control

A newer type of fly control is natural: It includes the use of tiny wasps that consume fly pupae. The wasps are completely harmless to humans and horses. They are routinely delivered in the form of cocoons, which are refrigerated to prevent hatching before they are used.

Each cocoon is about the size of a mouse dropping and yields from twenty to forty wasps. Once a week they are sprinkled from a container onto manure piles and dunging areas. To capture flies that come from neighboring farms, a pheromone, or hormone that attracts flies, is put into a fly trap.

An equine veterinarian who has been using this method of fly control on his small Michigan farm for several years raves about the system, and says it's less costly than traditional methods of control. Traditional pesticides cannot be used with the biological products; the chemicals would kill the wasps. However, the wasps work so well that he hasn't needed traditional sprays. The veterinarian buys the wasps from a company called Praxis (Allegan, MI).

This is the type of fly-control system that would have to be agreed upon and used by the barn owners and everyone who boards there. If you have horse or cattle farms nearby that don't have a good fly-control system in place, it may not work as well because flies from those farms may find their way to your horses, despite the fly traps.

Cold-Weather Care

Besides protecting horses from the elements by either stalling, providing outdoor shelters, or blanketing when appropriate, it's also important to warm up horses before riding them in cold weather. A horse who isn't adequately warmed up before a workout is more likely to injure himself.

When it's frigid outside, tack him up, but walk him by hand before mounting. If it's so cold that your horse has his tail tucked tightly against his body, walk him until that tail relaxes.

After mounting, walk for a good 10 minutes or so on level ground before trotting, and continue to take it easy for another 10 minutes, especially if you're riding an older horse.

Watch the footing. Avoid working a horse on muddy or icy ground. The horse could slip and injure himself. Avoid working a horse on ground that's very hard; it can injure his feet and legs.

Also take care not to put a freezing cold bit in a horse's mouth. If the bit is very cold, warm it to a comfortable temperature under hot water or in a heated room before using.

Cold-Weather Watering

It's just as important for horses to drink water in the winter as it is in summer. Some horses don't like to drink frigid water, and if the water in their bucket or tub freezes, they can't get to it. Sometimes in winter when the weather is very bad, horses don't get ridden or turned out as much, and without exercise they aren't as likely to drink. All these factors contribute to reduced water consumption, which in turn can lead to constipation and impactions.

Monitor water consumption carefully in cold weather. If freezing water is a problem, it may be necessary to get either a heater or a thermal bucket for the stall. Also place heaters in outdoor water tubs if the horses are going to be outdoors for more than a few hours daily.

If a horse doesn't seem to like drinking very cold water, try supplying him with warm water. During the coldest days of the year, I bring a couple of thermoses with boiling hot water to the barn and use it to heat up the cold water in my horse's bucket. It encourages him to drink.

Some owners also add a few pinches of salt to the horse's grain to encourage water drinking in cold weather.

Hot-Weather Care

Heat exhaustion or heat stroke is a potential problem in horses worked in hot, humid weather. They are more likely to develop these conditions if they aren't in good shape to begin with and are worked hard.

During hot summer months, try to ride in the evening or early morning. Offer the horse water periodically (only small amounts at a time).

You must take very special care if you trailer a horse in hot weather, because trailers get scorching hot. To prevent the horse from overheating, make sure the trailer is well ventilated and offer water to the horse frequently. Never leave a horse standing in a hot, unmoving trailer.

Cooling Down

Properly cooling down a horse that's been worked — in cold or hot weather — is just as important as warming him up before exercise. A horse that's not properly cooled down, especially if he's allowed to drink too much water, could develop laminitis and then founder. Founder is a serious condition of the feet, described in the next chapter, and it can be deadly.

If a horse is hot, his chest feels warmer than usual and he's sweating. To cool him down, untack him and walk him around until he has stopped actively sweating and his chest feels the way it does when he has not been worked. Don't let him drink more than a few sips of water until he has cooled down completely; otherwise, you increase his risk for developing laminitis.

In the wintertime, when it's breezy outside, put a cooler on him to protect him from chilling. If it's very hot outside, and you think he's over-heated, hose him on the neck and legs (inside the back legs, too). Don't use cold water on his back or stomach while he's still very hot; it will be very uncomfortable for him. You can sponge him or towel him off in these areas with tepid water.

Exercise

Moderation is the key. Be especially careful not to work a horse beyond his conditioning. A horse that hasn't been used most of the week must be ridden gently on the weekend; a 2-hour trail ride may be too much for him if he's out of shape, especially if you take him on hilly terrain, which is more strenuous. A horse in poor condition will breathe more heavily — watch his flank area to see if he's breathing hard — and will sweat more.

To get a horse accustomed to more vigorous rides, ride him routinely — several days of the week — and build him up gradually.

Some adult pleasure riders with busy careers just can't ride more than once or twice a week. If you're the only one riding a horse or have your own horse and you can't ride very often, just remember to consider the condition of the horse when you plan your ride.

Exercise and Food Don't Mix

A horse that is allowed to eat too soon *before or after* exercise can't digest food properly and may colic or founder. Both are serious medical conditions (see chapter 7).

Time your rides so that you're finished and the horse is completely cooled for about 1 hour before feeding time (although letting him graze or feeding him small amounts of hay after a ride once he's cooled down usually is okay. Just be sure to keep him away from grain). If he's already eaten, wait a good hour before riding.

Horse Illnesses and Ailments

7

Mary Wright grew up with horses, stopped riding for a while, and resumed the sport in her 30s. She rides almost daily during the summer months and at least twice weekly in winter. She prefers dressage and hacking.

"Riding provides a sense of well-being and accomplishment without peer pressure. It's fun, it gives me a sense of freedom, a clear head, and a chance to bond with the most beautiful beast God created. It's also something I can share with others who have similar interests."

IT WOULD TAKE A TEXTBOOK to provide a complete rundown of all the illnesses and ailments that can affect horses, but this chapter will get you off to a good start about important healthcare problems.

The goal always should be to prevent illness. Learn to differentiate what's normal from what's not, so you can readily identify a horse with a problem. That's what you'll learn about in this chapter.

Choke

This condition isn't common, but it's potentially quite serious and you should know how to spot it. Choke is much what it sounds like: A lump of food or a foreign body gets stuck in the esophagus.

Learning What's Normal

Learning to examine a horse is an important part of health care. It will enable you to tell whether a horse is ill. Veterinarians may also ask for information on vital signs when you make a telephone call to report a problem.

To learn what's abnormal, the best place to start is by learning what's normal. Look over the following list. Then ask an experienced horseman to review it with you and show you how to evaluate each of the following (with the help of a healthy, cooperative adult horse):

PARAMETER	NORMAL	HOW TO TEST
Temperature	99–101°F	You have to use a rectal thermometer. I favor the digital kind; it beeps when it's "done" and displays the temperature in numbers.
Pulse or heart rate	30–40 beats per minute	Find a major artery and use your fingertips, just as you would to feel your own pulse in your wrist. A major artery in the horse is located under the jawbone.
Respiration	10–20 breaths per minute	To check this properly, you need a stethoscope, which is placed on the horse's neck or on his side, over his lungs. For our purposes, watch the movements of the normal horse's nostrils and look at his flanks. Then look at a horse's nostrils and flanks right after he's been worked — he'll be breathing harder. If a horse is breathing hard when at rest, he may very well be sick.
Mucous membranes	Pink and moist	Look at the horse's gums. It's not normal for them to be very red or very white.
Capillary refill time	Less than 2 seconds	If you press on the horse's gums, the white spot left by your finger should return to the normal pink color in just a couple of seconds.
Intestinal sounds	Rumbling and gurgling	Put your ear on the side of a healthy horse, and you'll hear his gut working away. If you don't, or you hear an overactive gut, it could spell trouble.
Skin test for hydration	Skin bounces back into place	Pinch the skin on the horse's neck. It should bounce back into place immediately. When it doesn't, that means the horse may be dehydrated.

The horse with choke may stretch out the neck or appear to be straining; cough; exhibit drooling or saliva from the nose; and make noises indicating distress. Wolfing down food can result in choke; so can feeding rations that swell after they are eaten, such as small pellets and dry beet pulp. Choke also can result when a horse eats very fine hay or dry grain before drinking some water or is dehydrated; if a horse ingests something like pieces of wood; and if he ingests a piece of carrot or other treat that's too large.

A horse with choke may clear the blockage himself, but because it's a potentially lethal condition, call a veterinarian immediately if you suspect choke. One risk is that the esophagus will perforate, which can lead to death. The veterinarian may be able to clear the blockage by passing a tube to push the blockage on or to flush it out or may provide drug treatment that can help.

Colic

Colic is the leading killer of horses. It's not a disease but a sign of abdominal pain. The source of the pain can vary widely and could be due to anything from a simple case of gas to the far more serious intestinal blockage or twisting of the intestine. Unfortunately, horses that colic once are more likely to colic in the future.

Figuring out the cause of the abdominal problem and colic can be difficult. Internal parasitic infection is one culprit. Colic also has been associated with reduced water intake and dietary changes. Learn to recognize the signs, because colic is an emergency that requires immediate attention.

The signs of colic are one or more of the following:

- Uncharacteristic pawing
- Tossing the head or looking toward the flank
- Decreased (or increased) digestive tract sounds
- Reduced or absent bowel activity (no or fewer piles of manure)
- Sweating while at rest
- Lip curling or wrinkling up the muzzle
- Refusal to eat
- Odd standing positions, such as stretching out to urinate but not urinating
- Rolling or thrashing on the ground

▲
Tossing the head toward the flank area can be a sign of colic.

In its brochure on colic, the American Association of Equine Practitioners (AAEP) advises that if you suspect colic, remove all food and water and refrain from giving the horse any medication — this might mask important clues to the source of the problem. Be prepared to provide the veterinarian with certain information when you call:

- Pulse rate
- Respiratory rate
- Rectal temperature
- Color of mucous membranes (pink or white?)
- Capillary refill time (how many seconds it takes for the color to return to the gums after you press them with your finger)
- Behavior signs, such as thrashing
- Digestive noises
- Bowel movements, including color, consistency, and frequency
- Any recent changes in management, feeding, or exercise
- Medical history, including deworming and any past episodes of abdominal pain

When the veterinarian arrives, he'll examine and observe the horse. He'll probably perform a rectal examination to determine whether there's an intestinal blockage. Passing a stomach tube can help tell if there's excessive gas.

If gas or an impaction colic is suspected, a large dose of mineral oil may be administered through the tube. Painkillers usually are administered by the veterinarian. An abdominal tap might also be advised to help determine the severity of colic.

Mild colics often respond to medication alone, but more serious cases may require further treatment or an emergency trip to a veterinary hospital for further evaluation and perhaps even colic surgery.

Walking Colicky Horses

Walking a colicky horse remains a common practice. A little bit of walking might help the horse pass gas and feel better. But there are still many people who misguidedly want to walk a colicky horse to near exhaustion at a time when he needs every bit of energy he can muster to get through this episode of illness. Every time the poor horse lies down to rest, people start yelling, "Get him up! Get him up!"

Here's the reason that these marathon walks started: It was thought that if a colicky horse was allowed to lie down, he'd roll, which would twist his intestine and make the problem worse. This is now considered out-of-date thinking. Dr. David W. Ramey, author of *Horsefeathers: Facts versus Myths about Your Horse's Health,* puts it this way: "Just because a horse rolls doesn't mean he's going to twist his gut. And just because his gut is twisted and he happened to roll doesn't mean that the rolling caused the twisting." Horses roll all the time when they're outside exercising, and they don't twist their intestines, he points out.

The modern way to manage a colicky horse while you're waiting for the veterinarian is this: If he wants to lie down and rest, let him! If he starts to roll around violently, try to get him to stand up so he doesn't hurt himself while thrashing.

PREVENTION

Although the cause of colic is often difficult to determine, there are things we can do as horse owners to prevent this dreaded sign of illness. Here are several of them:

- Worm your horse regularly. Parasites in the gut can cause serious colic. An inexpensive tube of worming paste administered routinely can prevent parasite-related colics. (See the information on worming horses in chapter 6.)
- Make sure your horse has access to water at all times.
- Don't overfeed your horse, especially concentrates such as grain. Provide plenty of roughage, such as hay or pasture.
- Feed your horse according to a set routine. In a study conducted by N. D. Cohen et al. at Texas A&M University, a change in diet was a leading factor linked with colic episodes.
- Keep activity levels consistent. In the same Texas A&M study, a change in activity was linked to colic. (So was a change in stabling conditions. Consistency apparently is good for horses.)
- Don't mix exercise and feeding.
- Make sure your horse has ample turnout time. More turnout time has been associated with a reduced risk for colic. Horses need to move around. It keeps their insides working!

▲
Increased turnout time may reduce the risk of colic.

Eye Problems

In horses, eye injuries and eye diseases can be very serious, so any problem in this area warrants a prompt call to the veterinarian. A horse with a discharge from the eye or eyes or a horse that is squinting, blinks a lot, has a red eye, or that seems to be avoiding light should be checked as soon as possible.

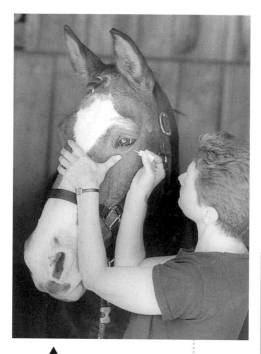

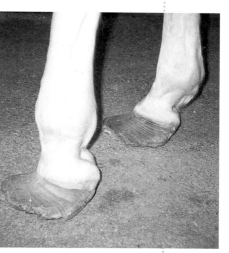

Eye problems in a horse can be serious, so call in a veterinarian if you suspect any trouble. If eye medicine is prescribed, check the label to make sure you're administering the correct product each time you use it.

Notice the damage to the hoof that can result from laminitis and founder.

Courtesy Days End Farm Horse Rescue, Lisbon, MD

Great care must be taken when medicating a horse's eye. If you apply a product containing corticosteroids to a horse with an ulcer of the cornea, the result can be disastrous — the cornea could rupture. Often, eye ointment is prescribed for a horse with an eye problem. The ointment comes in little tubes. Some of these tubes contain only antibiotics, but some contain antibiotics *and* corticosteroids. The problem is that all the tubes look very much alike. So carefully read the label on a product *each and every time* before putting it into a horse's eye to be certain it's the correct medication. Also, ask your veterinarian what the medication will do so you'll know in advance how your horse should respond.

PREVENTION

A safe environment that protects a horse from sharp objects minimizes the risk of eye injury. Protecting horses from flies is also important, which can help prevent disease, including some types of conjunctivitis (pink eye).

Horses develop some eye conditions that you can't prevent, but it's imperative that you seek early medical attention.

Laminitis and Founder

Laminitis and founder are right up there with colic as potentially serious, deadly problems.

It begins when there's a disturbance to the blood flow in the feet, which causes a lack of oxygen and swelling to the inner structures of the feet. This is called *laminitis*. Laminitis generally affects the front feet, and is considered acute when it's rapid in onset. Laminitis is considered chronic when it persists for more than a couple of days or if permanent damage occurs.

Horses with laminitis develop an odd stance to take weight off the painful feet by placing their front legs out farther than usual. If all four feet are involved, the horse may lie down or refuse to move at all. The horse also may have a high fever, diarrhea, and chills, as well as hot, painful feet. If the situation continues, the coffin bone of the foot rotates. Now the horse is said to have *foundered*.

Laminitis and founder can cause permanent damage to the structures of the feet, resulting in lameness. The damage can be so severe and permanent, the horse must be euthanized. Sometimes you can tell a horse has had laminitis and founder just by looking — he may have characteristic rings around the hooves, due to coronary band damage, and his toes may curl up at the ends, like elf shoes.

The causes of laminitis and founder are many, but important ones are too much grain, too much lush grass, and too much water when a horse is overworked and overheated. Overweight horses are more susceptible to founder, as are ponies.

Laminitis and founder are medical emergencies, so call the veterinarian immediately if you suspect these conditions. Treatment will vary, but the horse may require tubing with mineral oil if too much grain is thought to be a cause. Antibiotics, intravenous fluids, and anti-inflammatories may be administered. Special shoeing also may be required.

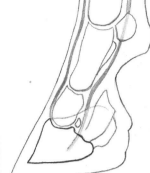

When a horse founders, the coffin bone, shown here, rotates downward.

PREVENTION

- Don't let a horse eat too much grain.
- Properly cool down a horse that has been worked by walking him until he has stopped sweating and his chest is no longer hot.
- Do not let a hot horse drink more than a few sips of water until he is completely cooled down.
- Restrict access to lush pasture, which generally is fast-growing, springtime grass.
- Don't let your horse become overweight.

Common Hoof Problems

You realize by now that for a horse to go well, he must have healthy feet. Then you're picking out his hooves, and you begin to notice things that don't seem quite right. The trouble is that when you're new to horses, it's hard to tell what's a problem and what's not.

Tom Parris, CJF, an accomplished farrier in Maryland, cites four conditions that commonly cause confusion and concern among new riders and horse owners.

1. **Thrush** is a bacterial infection of the foot characterized by a smelly black discharge that looks something like tar. It can be caused by different organisms, but the most common one is *Fusobacterium necrophorus*. Sounds ugly, doesn't it? It's more likely to occur if a horse's feet aren't kept clean, and especially when conditions are damp and dirty. A horse standing in mud all the time, or in a stall piled with manure and saturated with urine, is more likely to develop thrush than is a horse with clean, dry feet.

   Generally, thrush involves the central cleft (or central sulcus) of the frog, and the collateral sulci (see the illustration). Left untreated, thrush can become quite serious.

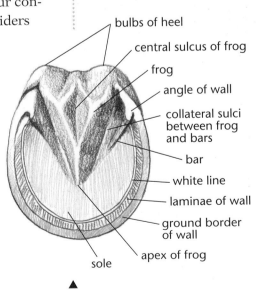

bulbs of heel
central sulcus of frog
frog
angle of wall
collateral sulci between frog and bars
bar
white line
laminae of wall
ground border of wall
apex of frog
sole

Parts of the hoof

It may penetrate and destroy the sensitive tissues of the foot. It certainly can cause lameness.

Often, however, when people encounter a smelly foot, they assume it's thrush although it isn't at all. It's simply manure packed into the feet. So how do you tell the difference?

If a horse has thrush, says Parris, the foot has a wet, oily feeling to it. "It's also got a rotten smell. Once you smell it, you'll never forget it," he says. If there's any question about whether a horse has thrush, he suggests washing the foot with soap and water: "If the smell doesn't come off, it's probably thrush. If washing removes the smell, it was probably just a dirty foot that needed to be thoroughly picked out."

Parris also suggests that you smell a normal, healthy foot from time to time, which will help you identify thrush if it does develop.

2. **Sand cracks,** or cracks in the hoof wall, are caused by several things. Dry conditions cause the hoof wall to lose flexibility, leading to cracks. A horse could have an injury of the coronary band that disturbs normal hoof growth, just as an injury to your nail root can disturb the growth of your fingernail. Another cause of sand cracks is an unbalanced foot, Parris says.

   "If sand cracks are no wider than a hair's diameter and are consistently the same width down the foot, they generally aren't a problem. If the cracks are wider," he cautions, "or they are wider on one end than the other, tell your instructor or the farrier."

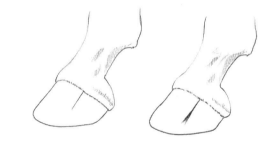

A crack no wider than a hair's diameter that's the same width down the foot usually is no cause for concern; if the crack is wider on one end than the other, though, notify your instructor or farrier.

3. **Chipping** is just what it sounds like: The bottom of the hoof wall chips off in places, leaving a ragged edge. "This is a problem only if the chip is deep enough up into the foot to cause bleeding. Otherwise, it's a cosmetic problem," says Parris.

4. **Peeling** of the frog and sole is something else you might notice when picking out the feet. This is normal and generally occurs twice yearly; it's a problem only if a horse happens to shed a particularly large piece of tissue and dampness gets underneath, Parris says. Leave minor peeling alone; the farrier will remove the sole and frog when he trims the horse.

There's one other question Parris frequently gets from newcomers to a barn. "When I'm nailing in shoes," he says, "they often ask, 'You mean that doesn't hurt the horse?' I assure them it doesn't — as long as I drive the nail into the right place."

Hyperkalemic Periodic Paralysis (HYPP)

This is a relatively new disease on the equine scene. It's a genetic defect and, so far, has been seen only in the offspring of an American Quarter Horse named Impressive.

There are horses with the defect that never seem to have a problem, but those that do can have attacks of muscle spasm, tremors, sweating, or paralysis that last from minutes to hours. Signs in affected horses can be triggered by management practices such as changes in the diet and water deprivation.

Some veterinarians say that horses affected by HYPP can be managed and ridden. However, there is a risk that a muscle spasm attack could occur while under saddle, so the rider should be someone experienced enough to detect an oncoming attack and able to get off quickly.

Rain Rot (Rain Scalds)

This is a condition that leads to crusty patches of skin that are often found on the back or rump but also on other areas, including the legs. It's the same problem that occurs in back of the fetlocks, which is called greased heels or dew poisoning.

Rain rot occurs in the spring, around the time when horses are shedding out their coats. It is caused by an organism called *Dermatophilosis congolensis,* which is described in various texts as a fungus or a cross between a fungus and bacterium.

Some people think this occurs only on horses that are poorly kept and inadequately groomed, but this just isn't the case. The organism that causes rain rot gets onto a horse (possibly from another horse or from a contaminated grooming tool). Moisture, as commonly occurs during the rainy spring season (when horses typically shed), activates the organism. Then the horse gets a break in the skin, which could be due to anything from a bug bite to a scrape, and now you've got a case of rain rot.

Sometimes rain rot goes away as the horse sheds, but sometimes it doesn't. Treatment is a good idea because rain rot can set the stage for development of a secondary bacterial infection.

Different methods of treatment are recommended. One is to lather the crusts with a cleansing product that contains iodine, such as Betadine surgical scrub. Let the iodine soak the scabs well, then work them off, which may cause the horse discomfort. You want to remove the scabs because they help the organism survive in the horse's skin.

Next, treat the areas for five days. You can use an iodine solution (Betadine) or Chlorhexadine. If the area doesn't respond, it's possible that a secondary bacterial infection has developed. The horse may need antibiotics, so call your veterinarian for his recommendations.

PREVENTION

Remember that rain rot can be spread among horses. Here are ways to prevent infection or reinfection:

- Try to keep your horse dry.
- Don't share grooming tools among horses.
- Disinfect grooming tools used on an infected horse by soaking them in hot soapy water with bleach added.
- Don't share tack, blankets, or saddle pads among horses. Thoroughly clean them if your horse has had rain rot.

Equine Protozoal Myeloencephalitis (EPM)

Don't even try to pronounce this; everyone calls it EPM anyway. It's a bizarre neurological disease that came to light in the past few years, and it is thought to be due to a protozoan that is transmitted by opossums. Birds also may be carriers, but their role in transmission of the disease is less clear.

A high number of horses are reportedly affected in areas where opossums are found. It is thought that an opossum excretes the protozoa in the stool and the stool contaminates the horse's food source, enabling the horse to ingest the parasites and become infected.

The signs of EPM are variable and can be frightening. A horse may become weak or paralyzed. If the midsection of the spinal column is affected, he may sit down on his hindquarters. Other, less obvious signs that have been reported include head tilting, facial paralysis, lameness, dragging of the feet, "roaring" or noisy breathing, staggering, and general lack of coordination. Some horses recover from EPM, some recover and then relapse, and too many don't recover at all from the initial onset.

To diagnose the disease, a spinal tap is necessary, but the results aren't always accurate. The clinical signs of the disease also must be factored in when determining whether a horse has EPM.

Treatment involves administration of a drug called pyrimethamine — an antimalarial medication — along with sulfonamides for several months, and it can be costly. Researchers at Ohio State University who are studying the disease advise that horses being treated for EPM also receive vitamin B–complex (folic acid) and that they be checked monthly for signs of anemia caused by the treatment. Anti-inflammatory drugs also are sometimes prescribed.

At this writing, new drugs are being evaluated for the treatment of EPM. To stay up-to-date on this disease, check out The Ohio State University's Web site (see resources).

> ### PREVENTION
>
> There is no surefire way to prevent EPM. It may be helpful, however, to prevent opossums from contaminating a horse's environment with their stool. This may entail setting traps to catch opossums on the property and keeping horse feed stored such that it won't be fouled. It also may be helpful to keep birds out of the barn.

Equine Infectious Anemia (EIA, Swamp Fever)

This is a viral disease that's been around since the 1800s. It is spread from animal to animal via secretions such as blood and saliva, by biting insects, and by contaminated equipment. It can be rapidly fatal. Symptoms include high fever, weakness, uncoordination, swelling, edema, and anemia. Some horses with EIA do not appear ill but are carriers of the disease. There is no specific treatment.

Very few horses in the United States have contracted EIA. However, because it is infectious and such a serious disease, most states require horses with EIA to be euthanized or permanently quarantined.

The test for EIA is called a Coggins. If a horse is shown or taken from one state to another, proof of a negative Coggins test usually is required.

> ### PREVENTION
>
> Protect horses from biting insects. Unless horses are kept in a completely closed herd (known to be free of EIA), it's wise to test annually for the disease. By identifying and removing carriers, the spread of EIA will continue to be contained.

Lameness

So many things can cause lameness that entire books have been written on the subject. Many instances of lameness, but not all, are due to a problem with the front feet and legs, where horses carry most of their weight, and problems in the feet are more often the cause than problems in the legs.

The horse may be just a little "off," meaning he's not going quite right or limping just a bit, to "three-legged, head-bobbin' lame," meaning he's so lame he won't put weight on one foot or leg at all and that he's moving his head to try to keep weight off a sore foot or leg.

Hoof testers aid in identifying a problem in the foot.

Picking out which foot or leg is the source of the problem can be tricky, and often requires an experienced eye.

For newer adult pleasure riders, the most important thing to remember is that if you're riding a horse and he suddenly starts limping, bobbing his head, or just feels "off," dismount immediately. If a horse goes lame and resists being moved at all, don't move him. Check for a stone or stick in one of the feet. If you can't readily find something to explain the problem, ask for help from your instructor or barn owner; he or she can help decide whether the veterinarian or farrier is needed.

When the problem can't be explained by a stick or stone in the foot, the horse must be examined for injuries to the legs or feet. Systematically examine each foot and leg and look for a wound, swelling, or heat, which can indicate an injury or abscess.

Hoof testers may be used to locate a problem in the foot. These look something like giant pliers. They are used to apply pressure on one section of the hoof at a time. If the horse responds to pressure in one area, which he may do by flinching, that indicates you may have located where the problem lies.

Two injuries to the feet that are common causes of lameness in usually sound horses are:

1. **Sole bruises and abscesses**. A horse may step on a rock and bruise sensitive tissues underneath the sole, which can cause pain and lameness. If an infection develops, the horse has an abscess.

   A horse with bruises or an abscess needs to rest the foot. The farrier or veterinarian may pare down the foot to try to find the problem. If an abscess is suspected, soaking the foot one to three times daily may be recommended — veterinarians differ about the benefits of soaking, but many still think it helps.

2. **Puncture wounds.** These can be potentially very serious because if an infection sets in, it can cause major damage and even destroy structures within the foot. A lame horse should carefully be checked for a puncture wound. Once in a while, the offending nail or staple is stuck in the foot and the cause of lameness is obvious, but more often it's impossible to tell with your eye that a puncture wound exists. If you see a nail or other object in the foot, let the veterinarian or farrier remove it so the exact location of the wound is obvious.

   As with bruises and abscesses, the horse's foot may need to be pared down by a veterinarian or farrier to find the problem (and even then, it may not be apparent). The area must be disinfected with a product such as iodine, and the foot wrapped. To keep the wound clean, you'll probably have to keep the horse inside and change the dressings to keep them clean.

   A tetanus shot is generally considered a must after any puncture wound.

Chronic Lameness

If a horse develops a continuing or intermittent problem with lameness, it's considered a chronic situation, and you need the help of a veterinarian.

A wide variety of problems can cause chronic lameness. One you're likely to hear about is navicular disease. It involves the navicular bone — a tiny little bone in the foot. It's thought to be associated with feet that are too small to carry the horse's body and seems to occur more often among Quarter Horses. Another condition that can cause chronic lameness is ringbone, which is an arthritis-like condition of the pastern or coffin joint.

Treatment for chronic lameness varies with the cause and may involve a combination of drug therapy and special shoeing. For example, one special type of shoe is the egg bar shoe, which — unlike a regular horse shoe — is a complete oval. It helps keep pressure off the heel.

With treatment, some horses can be kept sound and used, but others must be retired.

▲
This horse has had problems with lameness, and has on egg bar shoes to reduce heel pressure.

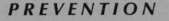

PREVENTION

It's impossible to completely protect a horse from injury, but you must do what you can to reduce the chances that he'll get hurt. This includes keeping him away from conditions that could lead to puncture wounds of the feet and legs. You wouldn't, for instance, walk a horse around a construction site where nails and shards of metal might be encountered, nor would you want to keep him in a pasture with a falling-down fence and exposed nails. Some types of lameness also can be prevented by proper care of the feet and hooves, and that requires regular trimming and shoeing as necessary.

Perhaps most important is to have any lameness problem diagnosed and treated early to prevent the condition from progressing to something more serious.

Wounds

Horses get lots of minor cuts and scrapes. How to treat them depends on whom you ask. One veterinary source advises using clean tap water, soap if the wound is dirty, and an antibiotic ointment; he advises against the use of iodine-containing products, which may damage tissues. Another veterinarian recommends an iodine-containing product, then rinsing, and then applying an antibacterial spray or ointment. Ask the veterinarian who serves your barn what he recommends.

My favorite product for minor cuts and scrapes is an antiseptic that contains iodine (VitaDerm), which is available from some catalogs. Wounds treated with this product seem to heal quite nicely, and the hair grows back well, too.

I still see a lot of people reach for a bottle of peroxide, but this is considered passé for fresh wounds because it can damage tissues. Once a wound is scabbed over, it's okay to use peroxide, then an antibiotic ointment.

For a wound that is anything other than minor, consult your instructor, barn owner, or call the veterinarian. If a wound is bleeding excessively, take steps to stop the flow immediately, until help arrives. You can use clean gauze pads, towels, or a sanitary napkin. Hold on the dressing with some type of bandage; an ace bandage or one of the products made specifically for bandaging horses, such as Vetrap or Co-Flex, will work well; both are widely available in tack shops and horse supply catalogs.

Here are some indications that a wound is more serious and may require attention from a veterinarian:

- Excessive bleeding
- A deep cut
- A cut over a joint
- A puncture wound
- Wounds over areas that move, such as behind the pastern or the hock

Be aware that horses are susceptible to contracting tetanus; if a horse sustains anything other than a minor wound, ask the veterinarian whether a tetanus booster is necessary. See below for more on tetanus.

PREVENTION

Keeping horses in a safe environment can help prevent serious injuries. Stalls and pastures should be free of sharp objects and barbed wire fencing, for instance.

Despite your best efforts, though, horses do injure themselves, so learn about treating wounds and when to seek help.

Immunization against Infectious Diseases

Horses can contract infectious diseases just as we can, but you can protect them from many by regular immunizations. Immunization against certain diseases is recommended routinely for virtually all adult horses, and is considered a crucial part of good horse health care. The following annual booster vaccinations are generally recommended for all healthy adult horses (immunization needs of foals and pregnant mares differ somewhat).

Tetanus Toxoid

Tetanus is the disease commonly known as lockjaw. It can be contracted by horses and humans (although it can't be passed between the two). It usually starts in a dirty wound and is due to an organism called *Clostridium tetani*. Horses are thought to have less natural immunity to tetanus, and therefore are considered to be at higher risk than other domestic animals for contracting the disease. That's why vaccination against tetanus is important.

If a horse sustains a penetrating injury, the veterinarian may advise a tetanus booster, which is a shot given in addition to the annual routine vaccination against the disease.

Eastern Equine Encephalomyelitis (EEE) and Western Equine Encephalomyelitis (WEE)

These are mosquito-transmitted infectious diseases that affect the central nervous system. Encephalomyelitis is also known as sleeping sickness. Horses may develop general signs of illness, such as loss of appetite, and then neurological signs ranging from difficulty in walking to paralysis.

EEE has occurred in the East and Southeast, and has a high death rate. WEE has occurred throughout North America, and about half the horses that contract the disease will die of it. Humans can contract the disease, too — from mosquito bites, not from horses.

Equine Influenza

Influenza is a contagious respiratory disease. It's airborne: An infected horse sneezes, and other horses catch the disease. The signs of the disease are a lot like the human cold or flu and include a runny nose, cough, fever, loss of appetite, and lethargy. Most horses recover just fine from the flu, but it can take weeks before they are back to normal.

The vaccine for this disease may not prevent a horse from contracting it, but should at least minimize the severity of the illness.

Horses that are exposed to horses outside the herd or that live in barns where any of the horses travel in and out should receive the vaccine, usually twice yearly. However, horses at higher risk, such as those taken often to shows, may need to be vaccinated as often as every two or three months. That's because the immunity provided by the vaccine is short-lived. Some horses that never travel and that live in closed herds — herds that are never exposed to incoming horses — may be able to forgo this vaccine. Ask the veterinarian — he will be familiar with the pattern of disease in your area and best able to make an informed recommendation.

Horses with flu should be isolated to protect other healthy horses. Time, rest, and good nursing care are the best remedy.

Rhinopneumonitis

Rhino, as this is often called, is quite common in horses. It causes symptoms similar to those of equine flu. In fact, flu and rhino cause such similar illness that it's nearly impossible to tell them apart without special testing. This disease can be spread in the air, but also by direct contact with infected water or other objects an infected horse has been around.

Rhino is an equine herpesvirus (EHV). There are two types that are of major concern in the horse, EHV-1 and EHV-4. In adult horses, both kinds can cause respiratory illness. EHV-1 can cause neurologic problems in adult horses, but most make a full recovery. EHV-1 is a greater concern to horse breeders, because it can cause pregnant mares to abort and cause foals to die.

Mares and foals must be vaccinated, sometimes several times a year. Many veterinarians recommend vaccination of healthy adult (non-pregnant) horses twice annually. If your horse is in a completely closed herd, however, it's possible your veterinarian will decide your horse can forgo this vaccine.

Isolate horses with rhino to protect other livestock. As with flu, time, rest, and good nursing care are the best remedy.

Antibiotic Treatment

Antibiotics are used for bacterial infections. Antibiotics are *not* effective against viral infections. Therefore, if a horse has rhinovirus or influenza, antibiotics are useless.

Horses with a viral respiratory illness, however, may develop a secondary bacterial infection, so antibiotic treatment may be advised by your veterinarian.

Regional Immunizations

Some diseases in horses seem to be limited to certain geographical areas. Here are some of the vaccines that may be recommended, depending on where you live.

Potomac Horse Fever

This is an infectious disease first described in horses living near the Potomac River basin in Maryland, but it has since been diagnosed in several other areas as distant as New England and California. It tends to be a warm-weather disease. Horses develop fever and diarrhea and other symptoms typical of a sick horse, such as loss of appetite and depression. Some horses also develop laminitis. Sometimes the signs of illness aren't so clear.

The organism that causes the disease is *Ehrlichia risticii,* which has been described as a cross between a bacterium and a virus. It is bloodborne, but how it's spread still isn't known. Flies, ticks, internal parasites, and even opossums have all been implicated.

Treatment for Potomac Horse Fever usually includes antibiotics, as well as fluids to combat dehydration from diarrhea, and painkillers if necessary. Horses treated early are likely to recover; for others, the disease can be fatal. Because signs of Potomac Horse Fever aren't always clear-cut, it can be difficult to get horses the early treatment they need.

There is a vaccine for Potomac Horse Fever, and although a study by Atwill and Mohammed questioned its effectiveness, it is still highly recommended by many veterinarians. Some believe it reduces the severity of disease.

Protecting horses from pests of all types, including flies, ticks, and internal parasites, may also help protect horses from Potomac Horse Fever. Researchers have found that the risk of exposure is decreased by applying fly spray daily instead of only a few times a week; by giving horses access to a run-in shed; and by deworming with pyrantel pamoate (Strongid).

Venezuelan Equine Encephalomyelitis (VEE)

VEE is similar to EEE and WEE. It hasn't been much of a problem in the United States but has occurred in Mexico. Therefore, experts advise that horses living near the Mexican border receive the vaccine.

Rabies

This is the same viral disease that affects dogs, cats, and humans, and it's usually fatal. Rabies is contracted from the bite of an infected or "rabid" animal. In some areas, rabies in the wildlife is a big problem. Where I live, rabies is widespread in raccoons, which poses a threat to domestic animals. In such areas, horses should be vaccinated against rabies annually.

Strangles

Strangles is an upper respiratory bacterial infection caused by a pathogen known as *Streptococcus equi*. Horses with strangles have general signs of illness, such as fever and loss of appetite, and they develop a nasal discharge. The disease is called strangles because it also leads to swelling and abscessing of the lymph nodes under the jaw, which may make it difficult for the horse to breathe. The abscesses eventually rupture and drain pus.

Strangles is spread by direct contact among horses, or by an object contaminated by an infected horse, such as a water bucket. It's a tenacious bug, and will persist on inanimate objects for weeks or months unless they are properly sterilized.

Penicillin is effective, but how to treat with it is controversial. Some veterinarians say that if penicillin is given once abscesses start developing, the abscesses won't abscess to the outside and that internal abscesses will occur. The condition is called *bastard strangles* and is very serious, even lethal.

However, Dr. Ramey's book, mentioned earlier in this chapter, says there is no experimental evidence to support the notion that penicillin treatment causes bastard strangles. In addition, if a horse has internal abscesses, the treatment would be penicillin. Still, he and other veterinarians say the best approach is to give penicillin before abscesses begin. If abscessing already is occurring, it might be best to let them rupture, or to cut them open so they'll drain and *then* initiate penicillin therapy.

The vaccine for strangles may provide some protection, but it is associated with a high rate of side effects — including abscessing at the injection site. Another potential side effect is something called purpura hemorrhagica, which is an inflammation of the blood vessels. This, too, can be very serious.

Some veterinarians believe it's safer to risk letting a horse contract strangles and treat for the disease than it is to risk the side effects of the vaccines against it. Others reserve vaccination for horses known to have been exposed to strangles. There's a potential problem with that approach, too. According to Dr. Ramey, studies show that vaccinating sick horses or horses harboring strangles in the early stages may increase the chances of them getting purpura hemorrhagica.

How best to manage strangles, in short, isn't simple and requires a thorough discussion with your veterinarian.

Equine Viral Arteritis (EVA)

This viral disease is more often a problem for breeders, since it can lead to abortion. It can cause respiratory illness in any horse, however, just like equine flu or rhino. If it's a problem in your area, your veterinarian may advise vaccination against this disease.

The Equine Veterinarian

Years ago, the local veterinarian treated all types of animals — dogs, cats, horses, cows, and whatever other creature needed care. Times have changed. There's so much information and knowledge emerging about different species that it's impossible for a single veterinarian to be well versed in all of them. Veterinary medicine isn't as specialized yet as human medicine, but it's getting closer every day.

To get the best care for horses, the veterinarian who treats them should be one who specializes in equine medicine. To find an equine veterinarian, ask many other horse owners whom they would recommend. If you ask enough of them, one or two names will keep coming up.

The organization that represents equine veterinarians is the American Association of Equine Practitioners (AAEP). You can find out more about the AAEP and obtain useful information about horse care by checking out the AAEP Web site (see resources).

When Is It Time to Buy a Horse?

Therese Sullivan rode throughout childhood but took a break in her twenties to start her family. She returned to riding at age 35. She most enjoys trail riding, her riding classes, and drill team.

"When I returned to riding, my children were taking lessons. It gave us an interest to enjoy together. Now the kids are grown and out on their own, but I continue to ride. It has brought new friends into my life, an opportunity to be outdoors, physical activity, new learning experiences, and many hours of enjoyment."

NOW THAT YOU'RE HOOKED on riding, and feel certain that it's an activity you want to continue, buying a horse is something you've probably start thinking about. Owning a horse is a major investment in time, money, and emotions, so proceed carefully. If you go about it in the right way, however, acquiring your own horse will be one of the most exciting and rewarding events of your life!

Experienced instructors agree that you should take lessons regularly for at least a year before you even consider buying a horse. By then, you will probably have gained adequate experience in handling horses, determined just what type of riding you want to pursue, and what types of horses you prefer.

Read over the information in this chapter and then decide whether horse ownership is right for you. Before you even start shopping for a horse, be aware of all the responsibilities: Think about where you would keep a horse, if you have the time it takes to properly care for one, and whether you can pay for his routine needs, along with some unexpected ones.

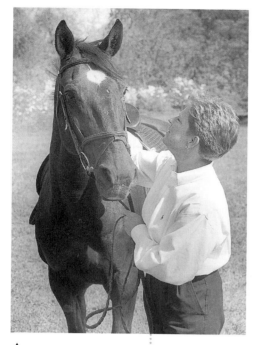

Go about it properly, and buying your first horse will be one of the most rewarding events of your life.

Owner Responsibilities

Owning a horse is a long-term commitment, so consider your ability to care for him not only now, but into the future. The woman who runs our local horse rescue takes in a lot of neglected horses and says most were owned by people who meant well, but "their circumstances changed" and they weren't able to provide adequate care.

If you want to buy a horse, you need to know the kind of person you are — preferably, it's the committed type. Let's hope you're also the kind of person responsible enough to know that if your circumstances did unexpectedly change and you could no longer keep a horse or properly care for him, it would be better to find the horse a good home rather than neglect him.

The Maryland Horse Council, Equine Welfare Committee, wisely points out that love just isn't enough when it comes to horse ownership. Consider these points from the council, with some additions of my own.

Do you understand and are you prepared to fulfill these needs? Horses:

1. Require a great deal of time and physical labor daily.
2. Require a great deal of specific knowledge for proper care.
3. Usually prefer the company of other horses over people.
4. Need food and water daily and, if stalled, their stalls need cleaning daily, too.
5. Need lots of exercise.
6. Can live a long time — some as long as 40 years!
7. Require an ongoing financial commitment.
8. Require routine veterinary and farrier care.

Where Will You Keep Your Horse?

As a relatively new adult rider still learning about horse care, you'll likely want to board the horse. You may be lucky enough to have your own property where you can keep a horse, but at least initially I'd strongly advise boarding. People newer to riding and horses just don't have the know-how necessary to care for horses properly. They often don't have the facilities they need, either.

Also, horses are herd animals and prefer to be around other horses; if you're going to have only one horse, chances are he will become bored and lonely.

The most compelling reason not to keep a horse on your own property is that it requires a good amount of hard physical labor and time. Weigh this fact against the cost of boarding.

It also can be very expensive to provide the facilities a horse needs. Maybe you have a barn on your property. If not, though, know that building one costs a small fortune. In my area, even a simple four-stall barn can run $20,000. You also need fencing and that, too, costs thousands of dollars; depending on the type of fencing material you select, it also may need maintenance. Even if your horse would live outdoors most or all of the time, you still need a three-sided shelter to protect him from the elements.

You already know that a horse must be carefully fed. Whether he is living outdoors some or all of the time, he still needs hay and often grain, too, especially when the grass isn't good. And when he gets grain, it needs to be in small portions at least twice daily. If the grass is too lush, you may have to restrict him from grazing, which could mean you need a dirt paddock or barn.

You must make sure your property doesn't contain any trees or plants that are poisonous to horses, such as black walnut, deadly nightshade, yew, and, sometimes, red maples.

Continual access to fresh water is crucial, so you've got to check, fill, and clean water buckets in stalls frequently, or fill outdoor tubs and clean them often, too. If you live in a place with cold winters and don't have automatic water heaters, you'll be out there in freezing weather breaking up ice in buckets or in tubs at the crack of dawn, midday, and late at night. Pastures need maintenance; stalls need cleaning daily and periodic repair; feed and hay must be purchased, hauled, and stored properly; the manure pile must be managed — the list goes on.

In addition, most people I know who keep a horse or two on their own property end up spending so much time caring for the horses and maintaining their little farm that they don't have time to ride. Nor do they have anyone to ride with.

Now, some people can learn all there is about caring for horses, have the property and facilities they need, do a great job of it, and enjoy it. Just be aware of all that's involved before you decide to keep a horse yourself. (See the recommended reading at the back of the book for more information.)

Considering all these things, it makes much more sense for many of us to board our horses at a facility where we pay someone who knows what he's doing to care for our animals. Don't worry — you'll still have plenty of responsibility. If you select the right boarding facility, you'll also have people around who can teach you a lot, and you'll have other people to ride with.

Time Required

The time you have to put into riding and caring for a horse should influence your decision about where to board him. If you have a busy work or family schedule and are pressed for time anyway, it isn't going to make much sense to keep your horse at a "self-care" facility where you're responsible for feeding, grooming, and stall cleaning. Owning a horse should be fun; don't make it a burden unless it's one you can handle.

Some full-board facilities will groom and exercise your horse, and you need to go out only when you want to ride, but these are expensive. At the average full-board facility, you usually are responsible for grooming and exercising. Count on going to the barn three or four times weekly. Five or six visits is better; three or four of those might be for riding, and the others to groom and be with your new friend.

On the other hand, don't make yourself crazy trying to get to the barn when you can't. We all have family emergencies and heavy workloads from time to time. Once in a while, we have to forgo time with the horse. That's the beauty of boarding. His basic needs will be cared for and generally there are people around you can ask to help with grooming and exercise. Sometimes, friends who are boarders take turns helping with each other's horses. If that isn't possible, you may have to hire someone to do it for you. When my work schedule gets so hectic I can't get to the barn, I have one of the barn's adolescent students help; I pay a nominal fee or buy a gift to say thank you.

The point here is to be realistic about the time you have to put into riding and caring for a horse. Factor it into your decision about where to keep your horse, because it will have a lot to do with that other major responsibility that goes with horse ownership — paying for it! During the times you just can't put in the time you'd like, get help.

Types of Boarding Facilities

Boarding facilities vary widely in what they offer, but here's a rundown:

- **Self-care.** You're basically renting space. It may be a pasture or a stall with access to pasture. Unless the owner is willing to strike up some other arrangement, you'll likely be responsible for all of the horse's care, such as feeding, turnout, grooming, and exercise. The facility may or may not be responsible for watering the horses. You may have to provide bedding for your own stall and muck it out daily. This kind of arrangement is among the cheapest, but it requires a complete commitment on your part. Come rain or shine, you need to be there to take care of your horse every single day, and perhaps twice a day.

- **Field board.** The horse is kept in a pasture. Watering, providing hay and grain, and checking the horses daily for injuries often is done for you. A well-maintained shelter to protect the horse from bad weather and continual access to water should be in the pasture. The owners may provide services such as blanketing and worming for the basic field-board cost or may provide these services for an extra charge.

- **Full board.** At most full-board facilities, horses live in a stall but are turned out daily. The barn takes care of watering and feeding the horses and cleaning out the stalls. Services such as blanketing and worming may be included in the basic board price, or they may be provided for an extra fee. You're usually responsible for grooming and exercising your horse.

Cost

Every time someone buys a horse at the barn where I ride, a lovely British woman named Mary enthusiastically offers hearty congratulations and says, "Welcome to empty pockets!" She's right. Owning a horse can be an expensive endeavor.

For me, it's meant keeping a car a few years longer than I might otherwise — the monthly cost of owning a horse is just about equivalent to a car payment — and I have to watch what I spend on clothes and on meals out. It's definitely meant some sacrifices. A bunch of us were lamenting the costs and the sacrifices one day, and my instructor asked, "But would you have it any other way?"

Unequivocally, no. I'd much prefer to be at the barn with my horse, riding with friends on a beautiful summer evening, than be in a new car dressed for dinner at a fancy restaurant. The people at the barn where I ride are all of modest means; we have to work hard to keep our horses, but I seldom hear complaints. In fact, I think we all feel privileged that we're able to own horses. It's a way of life, and owning a horse to many of us is the ultimate luxury. Decide if it's the way you want to live. You must be able to decide for yourself whether you can and want to handle the expense.

The initial cost of buying a horse is a one-shot deal. Most adult pleasure riders I know buying their first horse pay somewhere in the neighborhood of $2,000 to $4,000. You could pay less, or a very lot more. Then there's the purchase of tack and equipment. But these also are one-time or once-in-a-while expenses. It's the cost of upkeep you need to focus on.

Upkeep

Besides the basic boarding rate, some barns charge "à la carte" for other services, such as blanketing, medicating, and giving supplements; at other barns, board includes these services. Some barns include worming your horse in the price of the board; others require you to worm your own.

To give you an idea of just what's involved, in appendix A I've listed the average costs for horses boarded at two types of facilities. One is full-boarded at a barn in suburban Washington, D.C.; the other is field-boarded at a place about an hour outside the city. Of course, prices on boarding and other expenses will vary depending on where you live. Prices may be somewhat higher within a city, and they are a good bit lower in a rural area.

The full-board facility includes feeding, stall cleaning, and daily turnout. It's not a fancy barn, but it has an indoor ring, outdoor ring, fields, and direct access to limited trails. In my area, it's a middle-of-the-road barn — a friendly but average facility. There are some extra, à la carte charges.

The field-board facility is a small family farm. There are plenty of fields to ride in, somewhat indirect access to trails, no indoor ring, and few other boarders to ride with. There are several advantages at such a farm, though, that make up for the lack of facilities. The owner offers "flexible" board: If the weather is bad, she brings the horses into her barn and charges boarders a few dollars extra per night. She also provides other services for the basic boarding charge, such as blanketing, and offers plenty of TLC. You'll see in appendix A that the costs of full-board and field-board facilities differ significantly.

Add to boarding expenses the cost for the unexpected. Many horses need an extra visit or two annually from the veterinarian for injuries or occasional bouts of illness. Your farrier bill might also be much more if your horse requires special shoeing. And don't forget the cost of lessons — that may be another ongoing expense for you.

Now that you've got a good handle on everything that's involved in owning a horse, let's talk about buying one!

Where to Shop for a Horse

As a novice, you must enlist the help of someone who knows more than you do to shop and buy. Your best bets are the instructors, trainers, or owners at the barn where you've been riding as a student. Many sell horses themselves, and let's hope you've already come to like and trust them. Look around and ask others who have bought horses from them whether they think they got a good deal. Your instructor or barn owner might also know of other students at your barn who want to sell a horse and upgrade to another.

If you buy a horse from your instructor or barn owner, chances are you've already spent time riding that horse, or that you will be able to spend time riding him before making a commitment. Some barns will let you lease a horse you're interested in buying before you make a final decision.

At the full-board barn where I board, students who buy a horse from the owner are even given a one-year guarantee: If the horse doesn't work out for any reason, the horse is replaced! This makes us feel as though the barn owner values us as students, customers, and friends and wants to keep us happy. You probably won't find many horse sellers willing to give you that kind of guarantee, but maybe you can come close. At least try to get a trial period.

Although the place where you're riding may not sell horses, the instructors or owners are certain to know people who do. Ask for their help, because if you try it on your own, the experience could be worse than buying a used car. You can easily get into big trouble if you aren't careful.

Realize that it's harder to get a trial period when you buy a horse from a place other than the barn where you've been riding, and understandably so. If something happens to the horse during the trial, the seller has no way of knowing whether you or the management at the facility did something to cause or contribute to the problem. If you do get a trial period, make sure the terms are clearly spelled out in writing. If you have given a deposit, will it be refunded in full? Who is responsible for the horse in case of injury or death?

Auctions

Avoid buying a horse at auction. Auctions are the place where many problem horses are taken for quick sale. Occasionally there are some real bargains, but you also could end up with a disaster on your hands and a lot of heartbreak — either a horse with a serious lameness or other health problem that isn't readily apparent the day of the sale, or a horse with behavior problems. You just can't tell unless you're an experienced horse trader.

Another major disadvantage of buying a horse at auction is that you can't spend enough time riding him before you buy.

School Horses

School horses can be excellent first horses for new adult riders. Some people turn up their noses at school horses because they tend to be older, ordinary-looking grade horses, or mutts. They assume school horses are worked so hard that they're broken-down nags. Often this just isn't the case, especially if the horses have been used in a well-run lesson program.

"All things considered, beginning riders don't need a big flashy horse," says Tom Parris, CJF, an experienced horseman and farrier who works with several of the leading lesson barns in the Washington metropolitan area.

"In fact," he says, "school horses are the Cadillacs of the horse world. They are the best all-around horses. Yes, they work hard. But in my experience, they're well treated and cared for. They're also sane and steady. For the beginning adult rider looking for a safe, reliable horse, a school horse often is a perfect choice."

In short, school horses are tried-and-true. If they've been safe and sound for months or years in a lesson program, chances are they'll be as safe and sound as a privately owned horse. There's far less chance that you'll end up with a horse that's ornery — or that goes lame.

Classified Ads

Other places where you can shop include local horse publications, which are filled with ads of horses for sale by horse traders and average horse owners, and the Internet. Again, ask your instructor, trainer, or barn owner to go with you to check out any horse you're seriously interested in.

Some people shop long-distance for horses. They obtain a videotape of the horse, and decide based on the tape and talking to the owners. I'm not enthusiastic about long-distance horse shopping, especially for a novice; as I said above, you should have the opportunity to spend lots of time with a horse before you buy him. That's hard to do if he's not local.

A Sorry Horse Tale

An old horse trader named Walt wanted to sell a horse, so he ran an ad in the paper. He got a phone call from a guy asking if the horse could canter and if he'd go through water. "Sure," said Walt. The man wanted to come and see Walt's horse, and Walt said okay, but cautioned the man that the horse didn't look so good.

The man came out to see the horse, loved him, and bought him. He took the horse out on the trail, and the horse kept running into trees. He called Walt and said he thought the horse was blind, and wanted Walt to take the horse back. Walt wouldn't, so the man took Walt to court.

The judge asked Walt if he sold a blind horse to the man without telling him. Walt said, "Well, Your Honor, I told him the horse didn't look so good."

Temperament

Make good temperament, not the horse's appearance, your top priority. We all would enjoy having a gorgeous horse to parade around, but if you buy a horse with a temperament that doesn't suit you, you'll get frustrated and maybe frightened, too, which can really put a damper on your riding experience.

To novice adult riders and first-time horse owners, Deborah Reed, Ph.D., an experienced rider and expert in injury prevention, says, "Get a settled, older horse, preferably a gelding." Older horses and geldings generally are considered to have more even, calmer temperaments than younger horses and mares.

Horse trainer and former instructor David Butts says to consider how the horse has been used. A school horse that "goes easy" despite being ridden almost every day in a lesson program will go even easier when he's privately owned and not ridden as much. He may be downright frisky.

"Take this into account," says Butts, "and remember that it's easier to speed up a horse than it is to slow one down."

Matching Personalities

Do ask your instructor, trainer, or someone else you trust to provide an opinion about whether any horse you want to buy is a good fit with your own personality, and listen carefully to what you hear. Some horses do better with a firm but calm owner; if you're the high-strung type, a more docile horse might be a better choice.

Checking Background

When buying a horse that's not one you know from the barn where you've been riding, make inquiries about the horse's background. I'd wonder about a horse that had been passed from owner to owner. Ask if you can contact previous owners to ask them about the horse's temperament; if the person doesn't own the horse anymore, you're more likely to get the truth.

Test-Ride the Horse

No matter where you buy a horse — whether it's from your lesson barn or elsewhere — be sure to ride the horse in all the situations you plan to ride him when you own him. For instance, a horse might seem calm and steady in the ring during a class, but he could be a spooky, nervous wreck on the trail. If you want to buy a horse for trail riding, ride him on the trail before you buy him. Conversely, a horse that's great on the trail may not take well to ring work.

Ride the horse with other horses around, and ride the horse alone (close to the barn) to see how he behaves when separated from other horses. I'm thinking here of a horse that everyone thought was a well-behaved, docile old fellow until a student kept him in the ring while the other horses left. The horse panicked, reared, and tried to race back to the barn.

Ground Manners

Don't forget ground manners. Some horses are well behaved under saddle but just plain nasty about getting groomed and tacked up. Therefore, groom and tack up any horse you plan to buy; see how he behaves when you aren't on his back.

If you plan to take your horse to shows, be sure he trailers okay, too. Ask the horse's owner to walk him into a trailer, if possible.

◄
If you plan to take your horse to shows, be sure he trailers smoothly.

Match Living Conditions

It's preferable to buy a horse who's been living in circumstances similar to how you'll keep him. A horse that's been living outdoors most of his life, for instance, might not like being stabled all of a sudden. A well-behaved horse that has been living in a quiet little barn might not be as well behaved if he's moved to a busy lesson barn with lots of people and noise around all the time; he'll likely adjust, but it may take some time.

The Horse That "Needs Work"

Don't buy a green horse or a horse that "needs work" unless you have the time and the know-how to train him, or unless you can afford to hire a professional trainer. It's easy to become so excited about a beautiful horse with potential that we overlook a lack of training and convince ourselves we can make him just the way we want him with work and in time.

Before you move in this direction, think long and hard about how much time you really have to put into such an endeavor, about your riding skills, or about your finances if you'd have to enlist the help of someone else. If you don't, you could find yourself with a horse you can't use for what you want to do. For busy adults, it makes more sense to find a horse as "ready made" as possible for what you want to do with him. If you have the time, money, inclination, and skill to train a horse, then maybe it might make sense to buy one that needs work.

Matching Breeds to Rider Needs

There are exceptions to every rule, but there are a few generalizations that can be made about the temperament of certain horse breeds and their suitability for different kinds of work. So when you find a horse you like, investigate the breed and breed characteristics. I'll provide a few examples.

Thoroughbreds are often considered "hot-blooded" because they generally are faster and higher-strung than a lot of other breeds. Some horsemen also believe some Thoroughbreds are harder keepers — that it's harder to keep weight on them — compared with other breeds. Thoroughbreds are used for all kinds of riding sports — dressage, jumping, and fox hunting, to name just a few. Because they're likely to be high-spirited, they may not be the best breed for a relatively new adult rider.

The Arabian is another breed of horse that's considered "hot." Arabians are known for their stamina and agility, and are popular among endurance riders. An Arabian is also less likely to be quiet.

Quarter Horses seem to have even temperaments, making them suitable for a first horse, and are highly versatile as well. Quarter Horses are used for all of the various Western riding sports, including barrel racing and team penning, as well as for racing and trail riding, and some of them are good jumpers. Many school horses are Quarter Horses. A condition called navicular disease, which can lead to lameness (see page 105), has been associated with the Quarter Horse breed more so than other breeds, but there are plenty of Quarter Horses around who are sound. Horseman David Butts says, "Quarter Horses can make excellent first horses. They tend to have great dispositions. They don't get rattled as easily as some other horses; they're good old boys."

If you have a special need for a horse with a smooth gait, consider a Tennessee Walker. This breed is known not only for being docile, but also for giving an especially smooth ride. A Tennessee Walker is not suitable for jumping, but the horse could be an excellent choice for elderly riders or people with back problems who plan to stick to flat work.

The Family Horse

A common dilemma among families with more than one rider is finding a horse that will suit everyone's needs. Say Mom rides, and so do the kids. But they can't afford more than one horse.

It's a difficult circumstance, and may call for some hard choices. If it's Mom who's taken to riding seriously and needs a more advanced horse than the kids can handle, the kids may have to ride school horses, not a horse that's too much for them.

If you really want a horse that all family members can ride, you need to select the horse that the lowest-level rider can handle.

►

A good family horse is one that all family members can ride safely.

Mixed Breeds

The types of horses I've cited above are examples of purebreds. They'll cost you more, especially if they come with papers. But the horse world, just like the dog world, has plenty of mixed breeds or "grade" horses that are just as worthy of your consideration and will cost you less, too. You can still get an idea about temperament if you can tell what breeds they're likely to be.

My favorite "mutt" is the Draft cross. That's a cross between a huge, cold-blooded Draft horse, such as a Clydesdale or a Percheron, and a smaller breed such as a Quarter Horse. Draft horses are cold-bloods because they are placid and sweet, despite their large size; when crossed with a smaller horse, the result is often a larger-than-usual-size horse (but not as big as a full Draft) with a great temperament and more agility than a full-blooded Draft. I've seen a few Draft crosses that are frisky, but most aren't. Mine has proved perfect for pleasure riding. Sometimes these guys can be stubborn and it's hard to get them to go, but they tend to be so sweet and safe that it's a personality trait I'm happy to live with. (For a more in-depth rundown on the various breeds, as well as some great information on how to go about buying a horse, see recommended reading.)

Horse Size

Is the horse you want to buy a suitable size for you? If you're a larger person, you want a horse that's big enough and has a build able to carry your weight.

On more than one occasion, I've seen novice adult riders buy horses far too small for them, just because they could easily get up onto the horse. That's not very considerate for the horses and it's hard on them, too. If your legs are hanging under the horse's girth, chances are he's too small for you.

On the other hand, there are some sturdy, rotund ponies and small horses that may be better able to carry more weight than a very tall, slender horse. Just be sure to consider your size and the horse's, and get an expert opinion about whether the horse is large enough to carry you. Generally, a rider should not weigh more than 25 percent of the horse's weight.

Conversely, if you're a very small person, an exceptionally large horse might be difficult to mount or too strong for you to control.

Horse Age

Longevity among horses has improved tremendously over the years. Many horses live well into their 20s, many more are living into their 30s, and some ponies live to be 40 or more. A horse that remains sound and in general good health can continue to work, especially if he is used lightly as a pleasure horse.

For newer adult riders looking for a safe mount, older horses are a better choice than younger ones. They're just more settled. My instructor advises buying a horse no younger than about 6. Virtually all of the adult pleasure riders I know, including myself, have bought horses ranging in age from about 10 to 15. We don't view them as old; we see them as in their prime, and they are giving us many years of riding pleasure.

Outgrowing Your Horse

Here's a hard truth. If you take to riding seriously, and especially if you plan to advance your riding skills, it's quite possible that you will outgrow your first horse.

That doesn't mean you should "outhorse" yourself with your first purchase. It means you may have to sell your first horse and buy another.

If you can't stand the thought of parting with a horse once you buy him, consider leasing a horse while you're learning, and postpone buying one until your skills are advanced enough to invest in that fancy dream horse you won't outgrow so quickly.

Assessing Health

A horse should look healthy. He should appear well nourished, not like a bag of bones. His eyes should be bright. His gums should be pink, and ideally his teeth should meet evenly. There should be no discharge from the eyes or nose. His hooves should appear to be in good shape and free of deformities that might indicate a history of serious injury or of conditions such as laminitis. A dirty hair coat alone isn't necessarily a sign of poor health, but the horse should have a coat of ample and consistent thickness, and healthy skin that's free of scaling, bald places, or oozing patches, which are signs of less-than-perfect health.

These are all things you can determine yourself, but there's much more to judging a horse's health. Ask the current owner for the horse's medical history. Ask specifically if the horse has had any medical problems, and especially if he's ever colicked or foundered. Horses that have had one of these conditions are more likely to suffer from them again.

Be sure to ask if the horse has had any soundness problems — problems with lameness. If a horse is lame, you can't ride him. Horses that have been sound are more likely to remain sound than those that have had lameness problems. Check out the horse's shoes. If he's got anything other than the usual horseshoe, such as bar shoes (horseshoes that are a complete oval), wedge shoes (shoes that are elevated toward the back), or pads under his shoes, be leery. These are shoes and devices used in horses with soundness problems.

Also ask about the horse's worming schedule; you want to hear that's it's been routine.

If you know there was a previous owner, ask whether you can call that person. Someone with nothing to hide should be glad to provide the number. If a horse has had some kind of medical problem and you aren't sure of its significance, ask if you can speak with the veterinarian.

Next, you need to consider the horse's conformation before you move any further toward a purchase.

Assessing Conformation

Conformation means the way the horse is put together. It's generally thought that if a horse has good conformation, he's more likely to stay sound, and also will be more comfortable to ride.

Good conformation means the horse's body parts complement each other and appear to be in balance. His head is well proportioned for his neck and his neck is well proportioned, too. His back isn't too long or short for the rest of his body. The more the shoulder slopes, the smoother his gait may be. His legs should look well proportioned, not crooked or misshapen.

Many horses, however, have less-than-desirable conformation that has no adverse effect on their soundness or the comfort of your ride. They just aren't as handsome as horses with better conformation. In such cases, conformation shouldn't be a major concern when you're buying a first horse. The temperament of the horse, good general health, and soundness should be your top priorities.

The type of riding you plan to do is another factor to consider when judging conformation. A squat, bulky horse isn't as likely to be as good a jumper as a taller, sleek horse, but if you're planning on jumping only low jumps, it might not matter much. As horseman David Butts points out, "You're going to learn more from your first horse than you're ever going to teach him."

Judging a horse's conformation takes a lot of experience, so here again you need to depend on your instructor or other horsemen you know and trust. Get a couple of opinions!

Horse-Buying Priorities

Here are the three top priorities when buying a horse:

1. Good temperament
2. Good general health
3. Soundness (no signs of lameness)

If you can find a horse that has these three qualities, you've done pretty well!

Prepurchase Veterinary Examination

This is an examination conducted by the veterinarian to help ensure that the horse is in general good health and suitable for your purposes. It's often the last step in the process of buying a horse: We search for a horse, put a lot of time into finding out about him, get other opinions, spend time riding the horse, sometimes lease the horse for a while, and then, as a last move, get the veterinarian to examine the horse just to make sure he's okay.

I sometimes think we go about this prepurchase veterinary examination backwards. Often, by the time we call in the veterinarian, we've become so attached to the horse that we'd buy him even if the doctor told us he had six weeks to live. At the very least, we're heartbroken if the horse doesn't "vet out."

Considering that the cost of a prepurchase exam is often under $100 — next to nothing compared with the overall investment we make in a horse — it might make more sense to bring in the veterinarian much earlier in the game, especially if you're the kind of person who forms strong attachments to animals. I'll leave it to you to decide.

Do, however, get that prepurchase examination from an equine veterinarian, or a veterinarian who specializes in horses. Get recommendations from other horse owners about which veterinarians they would recommend to conduct such an examination, because some veterinarians are more experienced with prepurchase exams than others. Some even specialize within their specialty — they may be expert in examining ponies, for instance, or certain breeds of horses.

There is no standard way to conduct a prepurchase exam. It's going to vary with the veterinarian and the way you plan to use the horse. Here's a list of what may be done, however, according to the American Association of Equine Practitioners (AAEP):

1. Review the horse's medical history with the owner/agent, including vaccination and deworming schedules, feeding, and any supplements or drugs.
2. Check pulse, respiration, and temperature.
3. Listen to the heart and lungs.
4. Check nostrils, ears, and eyes.
5. Evaluate conformation.
6. Palpate body and limbs.
7. Draw blood sample for Coggins and possibly other tests.
8. Evaluate feet visually and with hoof testers.
9. Watch horse travel in a straight line, in small circles, and under saddle, preferably at the walk, trot, and canter, and preferably before the horse has been warmed up.
10. Perform flexion tests on joints.
11. Observe horse's behavior.

If the horse is to be used strictly for pleasure and there's nothing else indicating that the horse may have a lameness problem, it is unlikely the veterinarian will recommend X-raying the front feet, legs, or hocks. X rays might be recommended for a horse that will be used for jumping or some other sport that's more stressful on the joints. So might other tests, such as tests for drugs that may mask lameness, if you or the veterinarian suspects a problem and you want to check it out further.

Remember, novices should *not* buy a horse from someone they don't know and trust. The longer you've known the horse, the better.

"Vetting Out"

In its brochure on prepurchase exams, the AAEP points out that veterinarians aren't supposed to "pass or fail" a horse, although owners often interpret the results as just that. The veterinarian is supposed to provide you with information about any medical problems and explain the possibility for future problems in light of the horse's planned use.

It's understandable that veterinarians shy away from passing or failing a horse, because there are no guarantees when it comes to horses. I recall a beautiful Thoroughbred that "vetted out" perfectly, then developed a serious lameness 6 months later. In another case, an adorable white gelding at our barn "flunked" the vet test because the veterinarian found evidence of ringbone and couldn't predict whether it would affect the horse's soundness in the future. That was a few years ago and the horse is still going strong, having fun with the family's two daughters and their mother (see photo on page 121).

In my experience, few horses are perfect and "vet out" completely. One of my horses, for instance, has a slight heart murmur. He also has an old splint, and his tail is crooked when he raises it. The veterinarian thought none of these things would cause a problem down the road; so far, none has, and I don't expect any will. You have to talk over the findings with the veterinarian and others you trust to fully assess their meaning.

A major consideration is this: If the veterinarian finds something that could prove to be a problem down the road, are you willing to continue taking responsibility for the horse? Any horse can go lame or get sick, but if you buy one with a condition that increases his risk for going "bad" or has a condition that could make it near to impossible to resell him, are you willing to care for him in retirement, or support him while you take the time to find him a good new home? I hope your answer is yes.

Vices

Vices are bad habits that horses develop. They also are called stereotypies because these behaviors are repetitive.

If a horse with a vice is housed and managed well, it's unlikely that the vice will impair his health; vices are more often a management problem. Before you buy a horse with a vice, however, be sure you're willing and able to place the horse somewhere where he'll be properly managed. Sometimes it takes quite a bit of effort to find a place where a horse's stereotypies will be understood and managed properly.

Here are some of the more common vices seen in horses. I've provided some detail about cribbing, because it seems to be the vice that causes the most concern among horse owners.

Cribbing

The horse hooks his front teeth on something like a stall door or fence board, arches his neck against the object, and makes a grunting noise that would lead you to believe he is swallowing air.

Some people think cribbing is due to boredom. Others believe it occurs when horses aren't able to forage adequately. Wild horses forage most hours of the day; stalled horses are allowed to spend only minutes or hours a day "foraging" hay and eating concentrated food.

Whatever the cause, once a horse begins cribbing it becomes an addictive-like behavior that's virtually impossible to stop, but understandably so: Research shows that when horses crib, they get a dose of endorphins, which are brain chemicals that make horses feel good (just as exercise is said to provide a rise in beneficial brain chemicals in humans).

Cribbing seems to bother horse owners more than it does horses. Some owners even resort to a surgical treatment that involves cutting nerves to the muscles that flex the neck. This seems ridiculously extreme: In most cribbers, none of the problems that result is insurmountable with proper management.

I don't want to lead you to believe that cribbing is an innocuous problem. It causes serious wear of the top front teeth, which some people fear will interfere with the horse's ability to forage and retain weight. Many cribbers with seriously worn teeth forage just fine, however.

Cribbers also destroy stall doors, fence boards, and other objects they use to crib. The destruction will make them unwelcome at some farms. An alternative is to put cribbers at a farm that, instead of wood fencing, has high-tensile wire or electric fencing (without posts the horse can hook the teeth on to). Stall doors can be purchased that prevent cribbing and stalls can be designed to be free of ledges on which horses can hook their teeth.

Some horsemen believe cribbing causes colic — they think the horse is swallowing air. But consider research by Dr. Paul McGreevy, author of *Why Does My Horse . . .?* When he X-rayed horses as they cribbed, he found no evidence that they were actively swallowing air; instead, the esophagus expanded, and the grunting sound was caused by the soft palate flapping as air rushed from the mouth to the esophagus.

Dr. McGreevy also showed that horses deprived of both cribbing and eating had a dramatic stress response as indicated by blood tests, but when they were deprived of only one or the other, there was no stress response. When they were deprived of cribbing by being placed in "crib-proof" stalls, cribbers ate more than normal horses. These findings, he says, indicate that cribbing is not a misbehavior but "an elaborate technique used to offset the inadequacies of a concentrated diet."

In fact, Dr. McGreevy thinks it may be better to let cribbers crib, as long as they don't seem to have a predisposition to colic. Provide a cushioned surface for cribbing, he suggests, as that will help protect the teeth.

I've found with my cribber that he's better off living outside most of the time, but if he has to be stalled, it's helpful to provide unlimited access to hay, which encourages him to "forage" instead of crib. To keep him from gaining too much weight and me from going broke, I bought a nylon cord and wove it through an existing hay net to make the hay hard to get out, which also keeps him occupied.

It is a problem if a horse is so determined to crib that he won't eat. Some horses will crib on the water bucket in their stall; in the pasture, they'll choose a fence board over grass, although this problem is more likely to occur when the grass isn't good. In such cases, it may be necessary to deter cribbing.

The most common way is with the use of a cribbing strap. This is a strap that goes around the neck, with metal at the base of the neck, that exerts a "nutcracker" action when the horse arches his neck to crib, discouraging the activity. It seems unkind, but it doesn't really hurt him, and when the horse drops his head to eat, the strap is loose so he can eat comfortably. I prefer a leather to a nylon cribbing strap, which should break if he ever gets the strap hung up on something.

▶

My cribber, Guinness. Cribbing needn't be a serious problem if it's well managed.

Wood Chewing

The main concern with wood chewing is that a horse will get splinters in his mouth or that if he eats enough wood, he could develop an intestinal blockage. There are some who argue that wood chewing, like cribbing, doesn't pose a serious threat to the horse's health and that the main problem is property destruction.

If wood chewing seems to be a problem, one remedy is to house the horse at a place without wood fencing or in a stall without any ledges where he can chew, much like the approaches mentioned above for cribbers. A stall guard or stall door without wooden ledges also might be necessary. There are various paint-on substances to deter wood chewing, but they don't always work.

Take care that a wood chewer doesn't have access to wood treated with chemicals that could make him sick.

Weaving and Stall Walking

A horse who weaves rocks from front leg to front leg. There is concern that he will stress and injure his front feet and legs from this behavior. Horses that stall walk pace around their stalls.

A horse with these behaviors may benefit from being outdoors more often and from more exercise. When stalled, it may help to keep him occupied by providing a tightly packed hay net as described above for cribbers.

Boarding Your Horse

If you've been taking lessons at a barn you like that also boards horses, chances are you'll board your horse there, too, and that's great. It's a place that's probably already begun to feel like home, and will even more so after you become a boarder.

If this isn't the case, though, and you have to find a place to board your new horse, consider many of the same factors you would when selecting a lesson barn, which you learned about in chapter 2. Is the location of the barn suitable? Are the facilities adequate for your riding needs? For instance, is there an indoor ring for riding in inclement weather? Is there easy access to ample trails if you're a trail rider? Following are some additional factors to consider in a boarding barn.

Willingness to Educate

Determine whether the people at the barn where you plan to board are willing to help you learn how to take care of your horse. I can guarantee that when you first buy a horse, you're going to have twenty questions every time you walk into the barn, despite what you've read and how much you've learned as a riding student. "Is this cut serious?" "How do I treat it?" "Is it okay to give him more hay just now?" "How do I put on his blanket?" "Does his eye look irritated?" "Do his feet need trimming?" The list goes on.

Some barns just aren't set up to handle all these inquiries from new horse owners; they don't have the staff, time, or inclination. A lesson barn that's geared to teaching, however, often is, because teaching is the mindset of the staff.

A lesson barn may have another big advantage. If you're going to need help caring for your horse — either grooming him, exercising him, or both — a lesson barn may have plenty of working students around. These are kids who help out in the barn in exchange for extra riding time. They are often glad to help you, too, in exchange for riding your horse, or for a nominal payment or a gift.

Free Choice

Ask if you'll have free choice regarding veterinarians, farriers, and instructors. Most barns I know allow you to use the veterinarian or farrier of your choice, but some expect you to use the professionals they use. Some even have a farrier "on the premises," which often is one of the owners. You might be perfectly happy using the same people they want you to use, but if not, there could be some conflict.

Some barns also expect you to use their instructors and would forbid or frown on your bringing in instructors from outside. Also, a barn's liability insurance may prohibit the use of outside instructors. So ask before you commit if it will be of concern to you.

Horse Care

Horse care should be a top priority when selecting a boarding facility. First, determine whether most horses there are healthy and well cared for in appearance. Check out the safety of the facilities. Look to see if:

1. Stalls, paddocks, and fencing are maintained well enough to keep the horses in and prevent injury. Barbed wire is especially dangerous and can cause severe injuries if a horse gets caught up in it, so avoid places that have barbed wire fencing.

2. There are well-maintained shelters in the fields if the horses are kept in pasture and aren't stalled.

3. The pastures are maintained and the grass is decent during prime growing season.

4. The horses are fed appropriately. Most well-run barns provide hay and some grain at least twice daily for horses that are worked, even if the horses are turned out to pasture several hours a day. The exception might be when the grass is very good. If the pasture isn't good, which can easily happen during serious summer droughts or in the winter, then the barn must accommodate the horses when they are outside with more hay; this is especially important in winter for horses living outdoors, as hay helps them generate the energy they need to stay warm.
   If the horses are stalled most of the time and don't have access to pasture often, they definitely should be receiving hay and some grain at least twice a day.

5. The horses are turned out. Turnout is good for horses. Grazing is good for them, moving around is good for their general health, and getting an opportunity to get out and play with their buddies is great for their mental health. Many boarding facilities, especially those in urban areas, don't have much pasture and horses are turned out only a few hours a day, but that's better than nothing. Some urban barns have no pasture and the horses seem to do okay turned out in paddocks with plenty of hay, but this isn't a place I'd want my horse.

6. There's a continuous water supply indoors and out. Indoors, the staff should check water buckets routinely, or there should be automatic waterers in every stall. Outdoors, there should be tubs of water or access to a stream.
   Ask how water is supplied during frigid weather. If there aren't water heaters, that means the staff has to routinely break ice in buckets, which is fine as long as they do it; if horses are living outdoors, there should be a tub with a water heater.

7. Stalls are cleaned daily. Stalls should not only be picked out daily, they should be stripped periodically as well. Once a week is good.

8. There is someone on the premises overnight. Many barns don't have the facilities for someone to live on the premises or can't afford to pay someone to live there, and the horses are well cared for. But I would prefer not to board my horse where no one is around overnight. When someone is there, it's more likely that an ill or injured horse will get help promptly. Ideally, the facility also would have a dog or two to guard against intruders.

9. There's a plan for worming horses. A schedule for worming indicates good management practices.

10. The barn hasn't had a history of repeated cases of colic, founder, or serious injury. You might get more accurate imformation about this from other boarders at the barn than from the owners. The larger the barn and the more horses there are, the more likely it is that the barn has had cases of colic, founder, or horses that have sustained injuries — the odds of these things happening are just greater. What you don't want to hear about is an epidemic of colic, founder, or what seems to be an inordinate number of injuries; this could indicate poor management practices.

Other Boarders

Meeting other people, having others to ride with, and building a social life may be important to you. Make it a point to visit the barn when other boarders are present, introduce yourself, and see what kind of reception you get.

I've heard complaints from people over the years that at some barns, there isn't much social interaction and that the people are "snobby." Often, the real problem is simply that the approach to riding and the goals of the boarders are different from people at more social barns. The riders at the "snobby" barns may simply take riding more seriously than at some other barns: They are there to ride, not socialize.

To avoid a bad match between you and a barn, ask questions. Is this the kind of barn where people get together to ride? Or is it a place where each rider tends to work on his own?

▲
If you want to board at a social barn, stop in when other boarders are there to see if they are warm and friendly.

Weigh the Pros and Cons

No boarding barn is perfect. You might find one where the people are nice and the horses are well cared for, but the facilities are less than optimal. Then there are fancy barns with every facility you can think of that lack the kind of atmosphere you want. Don't expect perfection. Weigh the pros and cons and make the best selection from the choices you have.

Insurance

One type of basic insurance for horses is mortality insurance, which pays you a flat sum (usually the price you paid) if something happens to your horse, perhaps less a deductible. If he's valuable to you, and especially if you couldn't afford to replace him, then I recommend mortality insurance. Some companies have an age restriction on mortality insurance, so if you want mortality insurance and have an older horse, you may have to shop around.

Another type of insurance is major medical. Policies vary among companies, but the coverage I have for one of my horses is limited to about $7,500 per year, with a $250 deductible per incident or illness. It provides coverage for necessary surgical procedures, such as colic surgery, and helps cover expenses for treatment of other types of medical problems such as lameness — once my expenses exceed $250.

There are lots of exclusions in these policies. Previous conditions are likely to be excluded unless they haven't required treatment for a certain period of time, and coverage for some previous conditions, such as an intestinal resection for colic, may be permanently excluded. Ask a lot of questions.

Considering the cost of specialized veterinary care, I think the price of the policy is reasonable. Colic surgery usually costs several thousand dollars. It's an awful feeling to have to consider forgoing treatment because you just don't have the money, or to know that providing the care your horse needs will put you deep in debt.

One winter, one of my horses managed to get a burr in his eye that was so tiny it wasn't readily detected despite several visits from my regular veterinarian. We finally had to call in a veterinary ophthalmologist, who diagnosed the problem and removed the burr with specialized, high-powered equipment. When all was said and done, the cost of this episode was more than $600. Sure wish I'd had that insurance, which I purchased soon after!

The insurance policy I have costs $220 annually for mortality and major medical, and I think it's worth the price for the peace of mind it brings.

To help ensure that anyone you do business with is reputable, be sure to ask other horse owners which equine insurance agents and companies they'd recommend.

Insuring Yourself

Your homeowners' insurance may very well provide some protection just in case your horse ever gets out and causes damage to someone else's property, but check with your agent just to be sure. If you plan on letting anyone else ride your horse, ask whether you need to get a liability waiver signed by that person. Again, your agent should be able to advise you.

Alternatives to Buying a Horse

After considering all the information in this chapter, you may decide you can't afford to buy a horse or that it's more responsibility than you want to take on alone. You still have these three options:

1. **Lease a horse.** Find another owner looking to share expenses. The two of you should get along well and thoroughly discuss such issues as riding schedules and care of the horse before coming to an agreement.

2. **Buy a horse and lease him.** This is the reverse of the above. Generally under such arrangements, you would have the responsibility for the horse's expenses, but would have help paying the bills by having someone pay you to ride your horse. The advantage to this leasing arrangement is that you'd have primary control of the horse.

3. **Join a horse-sharing program.** Unfortunately, these are few and far between, but they are a great idea. In my area, this kind of program is available at a local barn and is known as Equi-Share. People pay a flat monthly rate for use of a pool of horses. They can ride any horse in the pool pretty much whenever they want as long as someone else hasn't signed up first and the horse hasn't been used too much. (To protect the horses, there are strict limits on the number of hours they can be ridden per week.) The cost is less than boarding a horse, and you don't have all the other expenses that go with horse ownership, such as veterinary bills.

9 The Barn Community

> Jimi Akin started taking riding lessons at age 37 and prefers dressage and drill team.
>
> *"What I most like about riding is the good company of Scout — my horse — the fondness we have for each other, and the social interaction with my friends at the barn. I also enjoy attending horse shows and appreciate the hard work and successes of others."*

ONE OF THE GREAT ADVANTAGES of taking up riding is the social opportunities it provides. Through riding, you'll meet new people and find new activities to enjoy.

You've already read earlier in this book that some barns are more social than others. The owners and staff organize activities for students and boarders. If the owners or staff where you ride don't have the time or inclination, ask whether you can start an activities club or arrange activities informally on your own. With a willing group, there's no end to the events you can plan.

For Riders Only

Planning riding activities in addition to your lessons is a good way to get in extra riding time, build riding skills, and have fun. The activities in this section are for riders, but several of them are good spectator sports, so you can invite your family and friends to come and watch.

Riding in Formation

Get about eight or more riders together and organize a team that rides in formation to music. The more riders you have, the more impressive it looks. Riding in formation really puts your skills to use. You have to focus on the routine, on getting your horse to do what you want, and because it's continuous motion, you'll find you just do it! The team can perform during schooling shows and other functions at your barn.

To ride in formation well, the horses and riders must become accustomed to riding close together. Some horses just don't have the temperament for this kind of riding, but many do.

My team rides primarily in two lines next to each other, which also means we ride in pairs. We try to keep the same partners so the horses get used to each other. This eliminates the sniping that sometimes occurs when two horses that don't know each other are put close together.

To look good, the team riding in formation must ride precisely. Horses riding side by side must keep their noses even. The spaces between pairs of riders must be the same. That means focusing on your horse's pace. All this takes practice, and the more a team practices, the better it becomes. My team usually has at least four practices before we put on a show.

The difficulty of the ride can be adjusted for the skill of the riders. Newer riders should stick to walking and trotting; more experienced riders can incorporate cantering moves and even some jumping.

◀

Riding in formation to music is a challenge, and it's lots of fun, too.

Ask an instructor to act as coach. (Offer to pay a nominal fee per rehearsal to make it worth the instructor's time.) If you have enough people, organize committees to select music and to choreograph your moves. Dressing similarly — everyone in black pants and white shirts, for example — and using the same color saddle pads on all the horses really spiffs up the show.

There are countless routines that your team can perform. Here are just a few of the moves that can be incorporated:

Thread the needle. Picture two lines or teams of horses. Each line begins in the corner of a ring (see illustration) and rides toward the center. A horse from one line crosses just in front of the horse from the other line, and so on. The riders must pace themselves just so in order to cross at the correct time and make this move look good. Threading the needle also looks nifty if you ride it in pairs — two horses at a time from each team crossing two horses from the other line.

The comb. Two lines of horses face each other across the ring. The horses trot (or canter, if you're really good) toward each other, and the lines ride through each other. Keeping the noses of all horses in each line even is a real challenge.

▶

To thread the needle, horses from two lines cross in front of each other (left); the same can be done in pairs (right).

▶

In the comb, two lines of riders ride toward each other, passing shoulder to shoulder (left). The challenge with the pinwheel (right) is to keep the horses in line nose to nose.

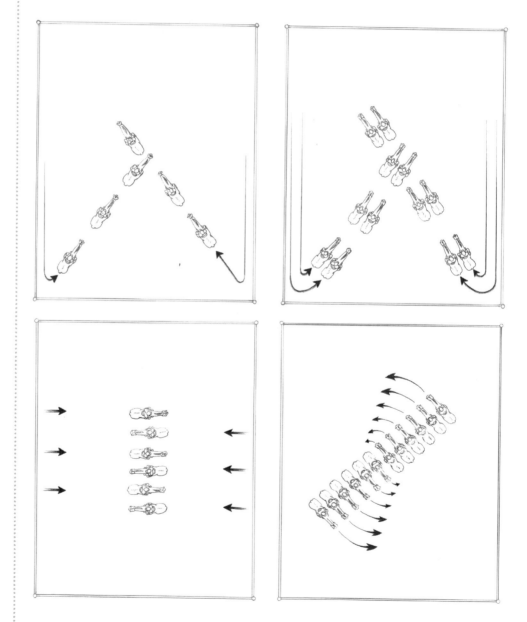

The pinwheel. All the horses on the team line up side to side, but half face the other way. The horses move in a circle while staying even nose to nose. This requires the horses on the outside to move faster than the horses in the middle, which move minimally.

Double circle. One line of riders rides in a circle one way and another line rides around the inside circle, going in the other direction.

Two circles. Each line of riders rides in a circle next to each other.

You can also perform "theme" rides. For example, at Halloween my team puts on a show for the children's Halloween party. We use music such as "Ghostbusters" and "The Monster Mash," and the riders hand out candy to children (over the fence) after the ride. At Christmas, we dress appropriately in red, white, and green and ride to Christmas music. At the end of the ride, we line up in two rows, and "Santa" trots down the middle of the rows on a beautiful white horse to hand out small presents to kids in the audience.

Organized Trail Rides

Weather permitting, you can organize trail rides around the barn every weekend, once a month, or seasonally, depending on the number of riders who are interested in participating. If there will be riders on school horses, check with your instructor or barn owner to determine the availability of horses and the cost for students using the horses for such a ride; the barn may very well also want to send along an instructor or two to lead and supervise the ride.

Determine the level of riding ahead of time. If the organizers of the ride plan to canter or jump logs in the woods, make that clear, because the ride won't be appropriate for beginning riders.

You can combine trail rides with a social gathering. Have an early-morning trail ride and then coffee and doughnuts, or plan on going out to breakfast afterward. Or have an evening trail ride followed by a party.

If your barn offers trailering services, consider taking horses to ride in new places. Where I live, we're lucky to have several nice parks with dedicated bridle paths. We trailer the horses there and enjoy the change of scenery.

Another option is to organize a trip to a barn that offers its own horses for special trail-riding trips. A retired history professor in the Washington area has his own stable and takes out groups of people in the woods along the C&O Canal. In other areas, there are stables that take riders on horses through historic sites, such as Gettysburg.

See page 140 for ideas for recreational riding trips.

Games Night

Adults enjoy playing games on horseback as much as children do. Combining a "games night" with a barbecue is a great way to spend a summer evening. Here are a few games you can play:

Scavenger hunt. This can be arranged in many ways. One is to give each rider a list of objects to find around a field and/or neighboring woods, and hints to help him find the objects. Objects could include horseshoes hanging on low tree branches, different types of leaves, or apples on fence posts. (Riders can tie a bag onto the D-rings on their saddles to carry their finds.) The rider who retrieves all the objects and returns first wins.

Tag. This is just like playing tag on foot, but it's played on horseback. If you're really daring and have riders with enough skill, try it bareback!

Spoon-and-egg relay race. Riders are divided into two teams. One rider at a time from each team has to carry with one hand an egg on a spoon across the ring and back. The team that breaks the fewest eggs wins. Try it at the walk first. At the trot, it's pretty tough!

▶

Adults enjoy games on horseback, such as the spoon-and-egg relay race shown here, just as much as kids.

Speed relay race. Riders are divided into two teams. One rider at a time from each team "races" from one end of the ring to the other and back and touches the next rider on his or her team, who then has his turn, and so on. The team that finishes first wins. To spice it up, require riders to circle a cone or two en route across the ring.

Musical squares. Set one-foot-square blocks of wood or tiles in a circle around the ring, about 30 feet apart. Put out one less block than there are riders; if you have ten riders, set out nine blocks. Play music. When the music stops, each horse and rider scrambles to get onto a block of wood. The rider who is left out is out of the game. Continue until only one rider is left. That's the winner.

Activities for Riders and Nonriders

An adult who takes up riding is likely to have a spouse, significant other, or children who don't ride. The rider wants to spend more time around horse-related activities, but feels guilty about leaving nonriding family members behind. To solve this dilemma, organize nonriding activities that everyone can enjoy; this promotes interest in horses among everyone — as well as family harmony.

Spectator Sports

Get on the mailing list of equine organizations in your area that put on events.

Many hunt clubs have "point-to-point" races or steeplechases each spring. Get a group together, buy a space on the rail around the field, and have a tailgate party during the races. My group plans a menu, and everyone brings an assigned dish and what he wants to drink, as well as supplies and equipment such as tables and chairs, napkins, and plates. Other groups with a grander budget hire caterers to feed them during the races. The cost of the space, tickets for each person, and other expenses is split among the group. We've been able to have a great time at these races for about $15 a person.

Local polo clubs put on games to benefit charitable organizations. These, too, are like tailgate parties and are organized similarly.

Have a racetrack in your area? It's fun to get a group together for dinner and a night at the races. Perhaps your barn owner or instructor knows someone who owns a racehorse or two. If so, ask whether a special tour of the facilities can be arranged.

Some of the larger horse shows also make a good outing for both riders and nonriders.

Charitable Events

Organize an event to raise money for local horse rescue organizations or equine hospitals. These events require tremendous planning and work on everyone's part, but the results are gratifying. They're also a good way for riders and nonriders to get to know one another.

You could have an evening party with dinner and entertainment, or a summer-afternoon picnic with games. The profit comes from two sources: One is from the sale of tickets, the other is from local merchants who donate items for a silent auction and raffle.

Parties

Take advantage of seasons and special occasions to get everyone together. A summer picnic or the Christmas season provides a great excuse for a party. My barn has an annual Kentucky Derby Day party where mint juleps are served; a television is set up so we can all watch the race and cheer on our favorite horse.

Ask someone to organize the menu and charge everyone attending a nominal fee to cover expenses, or make it a potluck-and-BYOB event.

Tours

Arrange for trips to other barns or horse farms in your area. Call ahead and ask if you can come for a group tour, and set up a time.

You can also make these kinds of trip on a smaller scale. I have a friend who is interested in Morgans, a particular breed of horse. For her birthday, a couple of us arranged to visit a family with a small farm that raises Morgans. We found the farm in our local horse publication. The farm owners were delighted to share their interest in Morgans. They also viewed us as contacts who could lead to horse sales for them down the road.

We've also visited a farm that breeds Shires, our local horse rescue farm, and a farm that raises miniature horses. The university-affiliated equine hospital in our area arranges for tours of its facilities. Look at the ads in your local horse publications; you'll probably find all kinds of places to visit.

A follow-up thank-you note or small gift is a good idea if the owners of a farm take the time to show you around; after a visit to a rescue organization or equine medical facility that depends on donations, a contribution is a nice way to say thank you.

Miscellaneous Activities

You're limited only by your imagination. You can organize ski trips, trips to a local theater, even shopping trips. Start by polling your group to see which activities would interest the most people.

Recreational Riding Trips

Recreational riding trips, including trips to dude ranches, make a great vacation for a group from your barn or for your family. Many outfitters (not all) that offer these rides are used to new riders and have appropriate horses. Some ranches also have other activities, such as golf and tennis, for nonriders.

Recreational riding trips are available in many places throughout the United States. With a computer and access to the Internet, all you have to do is conduct a search for "horseback riding" and you'll find lots.

The best way to select a place, however, is by getting a recommendation from other people, especially to make sure the outfit practices safe riding. At most barns, there are likely to be a few people around who have been on recreational riding trips and can make recommendations.

See the resources section in this book for a few suggestions.

Courtesy Outlaw Trail Ride

Courtesy Ricochet Ranch

Courtesy American Wilderness Experience

Want to broaden your riding experiences?
Ride the range, ride on the beach, or ride
in big-sky country. (See page 145 for more
information on riding opportunities.)

Educational Activities

Learning more about horses and horse care is another way to get people together. Check in your local horse publications, which are likely to list some of the activities available. Feed companies periodically hold seminars on nutrition. If you have a veterinary school in your area that teaches equine medicine, it also might offer seminars for horse owners on various topics.

Arrange for mini-courses to be given at your own barn. Ask your equine veterinarian to offer an hour or two course in first aid for horses. Perhaps the farrier can give a short lecture on proper hoof care. My barn sponsored a lecture by a woman who specializes in horse massage. These experts are often willing to provide this service for free or a nominal cost to build goodwill and promote their businesses. Or ask someone who's really expert at grooming or braiding manes to offer a short how-to class.

Most importantly, have fun! The world of horses can bring great joy to your life. Get out there and see for yourself.

▶

Arranging for local experts to give lectures to groups at your barn is a great way to learn more about horses and get people together.

Holiday Gift-Giving Ideas

It's traditional at many barns for friends to exchange gifts over the holidays. It doesn't have to be an experience that breaks your budget; small, inexpensive items in a 25-cent gift bag with a bow are fun to give and appreciated by everyone. Here are some ideas to get you started:

FOR RIDER	FOR HORSE
Socks	Hoof pick
Small box of horse-theme chocolates	Apple
Scented candle	Bag of horse treats
Tube of hand cream	Small face brush
Bath salts	Face sponge
Horse decal for car	Lead rope
Barn gloves	Portable safety hoof pick
Orange hunting vest (available at surplus stores for a few dollars)	Sleigh bells (for trail riders)
Sample bags of cocoa or tea bags	Bag of carrots
Glove liners	Rubber curry

Appendix A
Pricing Guide

BECAUSE COSTS AND PRICING VARY by state and location, this information is meant to be a basic reference only. At the very least, it will provide you with a starting point for determining whether riding will fit your budget. A comparison of boarding options and approximate costs for new tack are supplied.

COMPARISON OF BOARDING FACILITIES, SERVICES, AND COSTS

The services and pricing information for the full-board facility comes from a barn in suburban Washington, D.C.; field-board information comes from a barn one hour outside the city. Pricing will vary by state and location. (For more information about boarding, see chapter 8.)

SERVICE	FULL-BOARD FACILITY	FIELD-BOARD FACILITY
Yearly cost	$4,200 ($350 month)	$1,800 ($150 month)
Annual medication fee	$75*	$0
Blanketing (@$30 month for 3 winter months)	$90	$0
Wormers (every 8 weeks)	$68	$68
Fly repellent (summer months)	$45	$45
Farrier (6.5 times a year)	$280 (trim and shoes)	$143 (trim only)
Routine health care (immunizations, fecal checks, Coggins)	$121**	$65**
TOTAL:	$4,878	$2,121

Note: Costs in this chart reflect 1998 rates; rates may increase over time.

* At the full-board barn, all boarders are charged $75 a year to cover the cost of stocking the first-aid and medication cupboard for all the horses in the barn. It's easier than tracking and charging us individually each time an antiseptic or bandage is used on one of our horses, or if our horses have to have something like phenylbutazone, which is a commonly used anti-inflammatory. Boarders pay for all their own, other horse supplies.

** At the field-board barn, I take care of administering vaccines for my horse. That's why the healthcare bill is less than for the horse at the full-board barn, where a veterinarian provides all routine care.

STANDARD EQUIPMENT/TACK FOR YOU, YOUR HORSE, AND FOR TRAVEL, AND THEIR COSTS

EQUIPMENT/TACK	COST
For you	
Breeches/jodhpurs	$60
Leggings	$20
Protective helmet	$45–$100
Protective vest	$150
Riding boots	$40–$200
Riding shoes	$40
Riding tights	$30–$70
For horse	
Bit	$20
Blanket	$80–$150
Bridle (including noseband and reins)	$50–$200
Cinches, Western	$15–$50
Crop	$2–$4
Fly mask	$11–$15
Girths	
Leather	$30–$60
Synthetic cord	$15
Halter	$15
Lead	$6
Saddle	
Leather	$500–$2,000
Synthetic	$260–$500
Saddle Pad	
English	$25–$40
Western	$20–$200 and up
Sheets and coolers	$35–$100
Stirrup irons	$20 and up
Stirrup leathers	$30–$70
Whip	$6–$8
For travel	
Bucket	$10
Hay net	$4
Head bumper	$10
Shipping boots	$30–$50
Tail wrap	$10

Appendix B
Resources

Catalogs

**American Livestock Supply
  Horse Catalog**
613 Atlas Avenue, P.O. Box 8441
Madison, WI 53708
800-356-0700
General horse supplies

Boink
2333 CR 250
P.O. Box 4565
Durango, CO 81302
800-471-4659
*Sells tights in different lengths and
other riding wear.*

1824 Catalog for Plus Sizes
P.O. Box 293
Clifton, VA 20124
703-818-1517
*Good plus-sized breeches. Riding
jeans were rated highly in a survey
conducted by* The Perfect Horse.

Horse Health USA
2800 Leemont Avenue, NW
P.O. Box 9101
Canton, OH 44711
800-321-0235
General horse supplies

**KV Vet Supply Co. Equine
  Catalog**
3190 N Road
P.O. Box 245
David City, NE 68632
800-423-8211
General horse supplies

Libertyville Saddle Shop
P.O. Box M
Libertyville, IL 60048
800-872-3353
*General horse supplies and varied
riding wear*

Miller's
235 Murray Hill Parkway
East Rutherford, NJ 07073
800-525-6088
*Sells riding jeans that were found to
be favorites in a survey conducted by*
The Perfect Horse.

Praxis
2723 116th Avenue
Allegan, MI 49010
616-673-2793
E-mail: praxis@datawise.net
*Sells biological methods of control-
ling flies. Their Epona Kit, designed
specifically for horse farms, features
wasps that consume fly pupae.*

State Line Tack
1989 Transit Way
P.O. Box 935
Brockport, NY 14420
800-228-9208
*General horse supplies; also offers
tights, "full-figure" breeches, and
Western-style helmets. Specify either
the English or the Western catalog.*

Victoria's Secret
North American Office
P.O. Box 16589
Columbus, OH 43216
800-888-8200
Leggings and cami-bras.

Periodicals

The Equestrian Athlete
118 Lower Sand Branch Road
Black Mountain, NC 28711
E-mail: eai@circle.net
Web site: http://www.circle.net/~eai
800-404-8514
*Monthly newsletter for equestrians
about exercise and sports science.*

Equus
656 Quince Orchard Road
Gaithersburg, Md 20878
301-977-3900
E-mail: equuslts@aol.com
*News and articles about riding and
horse care.*

Riding Opportunities

**American Wilderness
  Experience, Inc.**
2820-A Wilderness Place
Boulder, CO 80301
800-444-0099
E-mail: awedave@aol.com
Web site: http://www.gorp.com/awe
*Prescreens dude ranches for every-
thing from safety to service and
matches vacationers with a ranch
that best suits them; publishes a
brochure of* Old West Dude Ranch
Vacations *annually, which contains
more than sixty of the West's leading
ranch properties throughout the
Rockies and Desert Southwest.*

Outlaw Trail Inc.
P.O. Box 1046
Thermopolis, WY 82443
888-362-RIDE
E-mail: outlaw@trib.com
Web site:
   http://w3.trib.com/~outlaw/
This nonprofit group organizes the Outlaw Trail Ride, an annual, weeklong event that takes place in August. It's better suited for those with some riding experience because the ride is 100 miles. It features fantastic scenery and, in the evenings, a campfire, music, storytelling, humor, local history, and good food.

Ricochet Ridge Ranch
24201 N. Highway One
Fort Bragg, CA 95437
888-873-5777 (888-TREK-RRR)
Web site:
   http://www.horse-vacation.com
This ranch offers a 7-day adventure along the California coastline and through the redwood forests; it also features overnight stays in bed-and-breakfast inns.

Web Sites

The number of Web sites that contain information useful for horseback riders and horse owners is growing rapidly. All you have to do is conduct an Internet search for "horses" and you'll come up with all kinds of sites to visit. Here are some of the Web sites you may want to check out:

The American Association of Equine Practitioners (AAEP)
http://www.aaep.org/
This Web site has educational articles for horse enthusiasts.

***Horse Illustrated* on-line**
http://wbs.com/www.animalnetwork.com/horses/index.htm
This is a horse magazine that has developed a Web site.

Horse Information Page
http://www.gac.edu/~mnichols/
   horses.html
This Web site is intended to lead you directly to other Web sites that contain information about the subject listed. Its creator says it's not as extensive as Web site directories, which are listed below.

Horseman's Advisor
http://www.horseadvice.com
This is my number one pick as a resource for up-to-date, informative, well-organized articles on horse healthcare issues. The articles are written by a veterinarian, and you can even send him questions (and get an answer)!

***HorsePlay*—Online!**
http://www.horseplay-online.com
Another publication with a Web site.

North American Riding for the Handicapped Association (NARHA)
http://www.NARHA.org
Offers information on therapeutic riding.

The Ohio State University
http://prevmed.vet.ohio-
   state.edu/epm/index.htm
An excellent source of information on equine protozoal myeloencephalitis (EPM).

Pet Care Forum
AOL users can access this site simply by typing in "pets" under keyword. Once you get to that section, go to horses. You can chat with other horse owners, ask veterinarians questions, access information, and much more.

Web "Directories"

The following Web sites are like directories. They'll let you see many horse-related Web sites, and you can access them by clicking.

Cybersteed
http://www.cybersteed.com

HayNet
http://www.freerein.com/haynet/in
   dex.html

HorseWeb
http://www.horseweb.com

NetVet
http://netvet.wustl.edu/horses.htm

USHorse
http://www.USHorse.com

Glossary

Anthelmintic. An agent that controls intestinal parasites.

"Barn sour." Describes a horse who would rather run back to the barn than work.

Billet. Leather strips on either side of an English saddle used to attach the girth.

Blaze. White on the face from forehead to muzzle.

Bots. An infection with the larvae of the adult bot fly. Horses must be routinely wormed to control this infection.

"Bute." Short for phenylbutazone, an anti-inflammatory drug commonly used in horses, especially for lameness problems.

Canter. The horse's three-beat gait.

Chestnuts. Horny-like growths on the inside of a horse's legs. They are thought to be the remains of the prehistoric horse's five toes.

Cinch. The device used to hold on a Western saddle that goes around the horse's girth.

Coggins. A blood test for equine infectious anemia, a potentially deadly disease. An annual test is often recommended for horses that go anywhere where they will be exposed to other horses. If you show your horse, and if you move your horse from state to state, you may be required to show proof of a negative Coggins test within the past year.

Colic. A sign of abdominal pain in the horse, which may be a medical emergency.

Colt. A male horse less than 4 years of age that has not been gelded (castrated).

Conformation. How a horse is anatomically put together.

Coronary band (Coronet). The area just above the top of the hoof, where the hair begins on the horse's leg.

Cribbing. A vice or bad habit that involves hooking the front teeth to an object such as the stall door or a fence board, arching the neck, and making a grunting noise. Although it's long been thought that cribbing involves swallowing air, recent research indicates that may not be the case. Cribbing is considered an unsoundness.

Crop. A short version of a whip, generally used to encourage the horse to move forward.

Cross ties. Ropes or leads attached to either side of the halter, preferably with panic snaps.

Dock. The solid, fleshy part of the horse's tail.

Equestrian. Someone who rides, or pertaining to things to do with horses.

Equine. The horse, or pertaining to the horse.

Equitation. The art and practice of riding a horse.

Ergots. A small horny growth on the back of the fetlock. Like chestnuts, these also are thought to be the remains of toes from horses of prehistoric times.

Farrier. The professional who trims and shoes horses.

Filly. A female horse less than 4 years of age.

Floating. The process of filing teeth.

Foal. A horse up to 1 year of age.

Founder. A condition that develops when the coffin bone, a bone in the horse's foot, rotates. Founder generally occurs after a horse has laminitis.

Frog. The triangle-shaped part of the bottom of the horse's foot.

Gelding. A male horse that has been castrated.

Girth. The device used to keep the saddle on the horse. It's also an anatomical term and means the circumference of the horse around his chest and withers.

Grade horse. A horse of no specific breed or that has no papers. The equine equivalent of a "mutt" dog.

"Green." A horse that hasn't been fully trained.

Hand. The way horses are measured. One hand equals 4 inches.

"Hard keeper." A horse that just can't seem to keep weight on despite a seemingly adequate diet.

Hocks. The tarsal joints of the horse.

Hoof testers. A device that looks something like giant pliers. It's used to apply pressure on one section of the hoof at a time to locate the source of a lameness.

Laminitis. A disturbance to the blood flow in the feet, which causes a lack of oxygen and swelling in sensitive inner structures of the feet.

Mare. A female horse over 4 years of age.

Martingale. A device to prevent a horse from raising his head too high or tossing the head up. Two common types are the standing martingale, which attaches to the girth and the noseband, and the running martingale, which attaches to the girth and the reins.

Neck rein. Reins are applied to the horse's neck to direct him.

"Off." Describes a horse that is a little lame and not going quite right.

Panic snaps. Attachments on a lead or rope that are affixed to the horse's halter. They can be released more easily, compared to other types of attachments, if the horse panics.

Poll. The top of a horse's head, between the ears.

Posting. Rising slightly from the saddle in rhythm with the horse's motion.

Ringbone. An arthritic condition. If it's in the pastern joint, it's called high ringbone. In the coffin joint, it's called low ringbone.

Ring sour. Describes a horse that has a bad attitude about working in the ring.

Seat. The way you sit on the horse.

Sheath. The pocket of skin around the penis.

Shying (Spooking). The horse is frightened by something and startles, jumps to the side, or tries to run away from whatever has alarmed him.

Smegma. A black, greasy material that collects in the sheath of male horses.

Sound. Describes a horse with no lameness problems. Soundness is also used to mean the horse has no vices, such as cribbing or stall weaving.

"Spooky." Describes a horse that shies or startles easily.

Strongyles. A type of worm that is a major threat to the health of horses unless controlled through routine worming. There are large strongyles and small strongyles.

Sweet feed. A loose mix of grain that contains molasses to make it more palatable.

Thrush. An infection of the foot characterized by a smelly black discharge that looks something like tar.

Trot. The horse's two-beat, diagonal gait.

Tubing. The administration of mineral oil through a tube run into the horse's stomach. This treatment is used sometimes for cases of colic and grain founder. Some horses are also wormed through a tube by veterinarians.

Turnout. Turning horses out into pasture.

"Vet out," "Vetted out." Horseman's lingo indicating that a horse will "pass" or has passed the prepurchase veterinary examination.

Withers. The highest part of the horse's back at the bottom of the neck.

Wormers. (Dewormers). Anthelmintics. They are used to treat intestinal parasites.

References and Recommended Reading

References

Atwill E. R., and H. O. Mohammed. *J Am Vet Med Assoc* 1996: 208:1290.

Cohen, N. D., et al. Case-control study of the association between various management factors and development of colic in horses. Texas Equine Colic Study Group. *J Am Vet Med Assoc* 1995; 206:667.

McGreevy, Paul. *Why Does My Horse . . .?* North Pomfret, VT: Trafalgar, 1996.

Richardson, J. O., et al. An evaluation of the accuracy of ageing horses by their dentition: A matter of experience? *Vet Rec* 1995; 137:88.

Rogers, Allison. "Ouch!" *Equus* 1995; 216:54.

Recommended Reading

American Association of Equine Practitioners. *Colic: Understanding the Digestive Tract and Its Function.* Lexington, KY: AAEP, 1994. *Brochure available from AAEP.*

Dawson, Jan. *Teaching Safe Horsemanship.* Pownal, VT: Storey Communications, Inc., 1997. *Intended for instructors, but if you want to know everything there is to know about riding safely, get a copy!*

Dutson, Judith. *Getting Your First Horse.* Pownal, VT: Storey Books, 1998. *Dutson teaches you how to be a smart horse shopper. The book also contains a great color section on breeds.*

Griffin, James M., and Tom Gore. *Horse Owner's Veterinary Handbook.* New York: Howell Book House, Inc., 1989. *A must for the bookshelf of any horse owner. It provides an easy-to-read rundown on horse illnesses and ailments.*

Hill, Cherry. *Horsekeeping on a Small Acreage.* Pownal, VT: Garden Way Publishing, 1990. *Want to buy a horse and take him home? Read this first. It will give you the run down on just what's involved in having a horse on your own property.*

Holerness-Roddam, Jane. *New Complete Book of the Horse.* New York: Smithmark Publishers, Inc., 1992. *Features a fantastic overview of all types of riding and is an excellent primer on learning to ride and horse training. It also features beautiful color photos throughout that make it a real pleasure to read.*

James, Ruth B. *How to Be Your Own Veterinarian (sometimes).* Mills, WY: Alpine Press, 1990. *Dr. James has written a very complete book on horse care and health. It may be a little too in-depth for novice riders, but those of you who are contemplating buying a horse or who have become especially interested in horse care should get a copy!*

Mettler, John J. Jr. *Horse Sense.* Pownal, VT: Garden Way Publishing, 1998. *A general guide to horse selection and care. Dr. Mettler includes some wonderful tales about working with clients that make the book a great read.*

Ramey, David W. *Horsefeathers: Facts versus Myths about Your Horse's Health.* New York: Howell Book House, Inc., 1994. *Dr. Ramey will set you straight about common horse health myths. Very easy to read and understand.*

Smith, Michael W. *Getting the Most from Riding Lessons.* Pownal, VT: Storey Books, 1998. *If you want to learn to ride the fun way, this book is a must-have. Smith provides step-by-step instruction with a sense of humor, and includes great advice about safety throughout. He also features a different horse in each chapter, so that readers really come to understand just what individual creatures horses are.*

Index

Note: Numbers in *italics* indicate illustrations and photographs; numbers in **boldface** indicate charts.

Other Storey Titles You Will Enjoy

The Basics of Western Riding, by Charlene Strickland. Gives new riders and those crossing over from other disciplines a thorough introductin to Western riding. Safe and effective horse-handling procedures and basic riding techniques are covered. Trail riding instructions and a complete guide to Western tack are also included. 160 pages. Paperback. ISBN 1-58017-030-7.

Becoming an Effective Rider, by Cherry Hill. Teaches riders how to evaluate their own skills, plan a work session, set goals and achieve them, and protect themselves from injury. 192 pages. Paperback. ISBN 0-88266-688-6.

Competing in Western Shows and Events, by Charlene Strickland. Focuses on Western horse show basics, the rules and players, showing for intermediate riders, showing your work horse, timed events, and arena exercises. 160 pages. Paperback. ISBN 1-58017-031-5.

From the Center of the Ring, by Cherry Hill. Covers all aspects of equestrian competition, both English and Western. 192 pages. Paperback. ISBN 0-88266-956-7.

Getting the Most from Riding Lessons, by Mike Smith. Offers valuable information on learning to ride the fun way, understanding school horses, and working with your instructor. 160 pages. Paperback. ISBN 1-58017-082-X.

Getting Your First Horse, by Judith Dutson. A comprehensive resource for first-time horse buyers. Includes information on choosing the best horse for you, boarding and care options, safety, horse health, and feeding. 176 pages. Paperback. ISBN 1-58017-078-1.

Horse Handling & Grooming: A Step-by-Step Photographic Guide, by Cherry Hill. Includes feeding, haltering, tying, grooming, clipping, bathing, braiding, and blanketing. The wealth of practical advice offered is thorough enough for beginners, yet useful enough for experienced riders improving or expanding their skills. 144 pages. Paperback. ISBN 0-88266-956-7.

Horse Health Care: A Step-by-Step Photographic Guide, by Cherry Hill. Explains bandaging, giving shots, examining teeth, deworming, exercising, and preventive care. 160 pages. Paperback. ISBN 0-88266-955-9.

Horse Sense: A Complete Guide to Horse Selection & Care, by John J. Mettler, Jr., D.V.M. Provides the basics on selecting, housing, fencing, and feeding a horse, including information on immunizations, dental care, and breeding. 160 pages. Paperback. ISBN 0-88266-545-6.

101 Arena Exercises, by Cherry Hill. This unique wire-bound ringside workout book can be hung up or draped over the rail ring for easy reference. English and Western exercises are fully explained, from the basic skills such as the working walk and jog to the "two squares" and "flying change." 224 pages. Paperback. ISBN 0-88266-316-X.

Starting and Running Your Own Horse Business, by Mary Ashby McDonald. This essential guide shows readers how to run a successful business and how to make the most of their investments in horses, facilities, equipment, and time over short- and long-term periods. 160 pages. Paperback. ISBN 0-88266-960-5.

Teaching Safe Horsemanship: A Guide to English and Western Instruction, by Jan Dawson. Presents a step-by-step teaching program focusing on safety lessons, boarding, showing, an guest ranch activities. Explains protective release forms, insurance, and dealing with an accident or lawsuit. 160 pages. Hardcover. ISBN 0-88266-972-9.

These and other Storey Books are available at your bookstore, farm store, garden center, or directly from Storey Books, Schoolhouse Road, Pownal, Vermont 05261, or by calling 1-800-441-5700. Or visit our website at www.storey.com